MANAGING
YOUR
MANAGER

MANAGING YOUR MANAGER

How to Get Ahead *with* Any Type of Boss

Gonzague Dufour

NEW YORK   CHICAGO   SAN FRANCISCO
LISBON   LONDON   MADRID   MEXICO CITY   MILAN
NEW DELHI   SAN JUAN   SEOUL   SINGAPORE
SYDNEY   TORONTO

1 2 3 4 5 6 7 8 9 0   QFR/QFR   1 5 4 3 2 1 0

ISBN: 978-0-07-175193-3
MHID: 0-07-175193-9

This publication is designed to provide accurate and authoritative information in regard to the subject matter covered. It is sold with the understanding that neither the author nor the publisher is engaged in rendering legal, accounting, securities trading, or other professional service. If legal advice or other expert assistance is required, the services of a competent professional person should be sought.

> —*From a Declaration of Principles Jointly Adopted by a Committee of the American Bar Association and a Committee of Publishers and Associations*

Names and identifying details in this book have been changed to protect anonymity.

Library of Congress Cataloging-in-Publication Data

Dufour, Gonzague.
  Managing your manager : how to get ahead with any type of boss / by Gonzague Dufour.
    p. cm.
  Includes index.
  ISBN 978-0-07-175193-3 (alk. paper)
  1. Managing your boss. 2. Interpersonal relations. I. Title.
  HF5548.83.D84 2011
  650.1'3–dc22

                                                          2010036609

McGraw-Hill books are available at special quantity discounts to use as premiums and sales promotions or for use in corporate training programs. To contact a representative, please e-mail us at bulksales@mcgraw-hill.com.

To Jacky, who knows so well the corporate world.

CONTENTS

CHAPTER 6

THE NAVEL
Challenge Your Own Values
119

CHAPTER 7

SITUATIONAL MANAGEMENT
Tailoring Your Boss Management to Events,
Moods, and Other Matters
141

CHAPTER 8

MANAGING OTHER TYPES OF BOSSES
169

CHAPTER 9

THE SEVENTH LEADER
191

ACKNOWLEDGMENTS

Thank you to Bruce Wexliar; without your support this book wouldn't have been that good.

INTRODUCTION

"How can I deal with my boss?"

I've probably asked myself this question hundreds of times over the course of my career, and I suspect you've done the same. It is a question we ask not only when we're frustrated by someone who we view as a "bad" boss, but when we're trying to help a "good" boss do the right thing.

It's also a question we're asking more now than ever before.

This is a time of tremendous stress in most workplaces. Organizations are pressuring managers to deliver better results with fewer people; they're asking them to work in new, flattened structures; they're insisting on diversity initiatives; they're rotating people in and out of groups frequently; and they're introducing new technologies that take some (or a lot of) getting used to.

In the best of environments, bosses can be challenging to deal with. In the worst of environments, they can be more than challenging—frustrating, perplexing, aggravating, and impossible.

Yet they can be managed. If there's one thing I've learned working for and observing many different bosses, it's that the right approach usually pays off in much more positive, productive relationships. "Right approach" are the key words. Your approach must be researched, planned, and executed properly. Most important of all, you must know your market. In this instance, knowing your market translates into understanding your boss type.

More specifically, understanding the six most common boss types: the Bully, the Good, the Kaleidoscope, the Star, the Scientist, and the Navel. I realize that many of these terms probably aren't familiar to you (at least when it comes to describing managers), but as you read about them, these archetypal bosses will become instantly recognizable. The odds are that you have, had, or will have at least one of these managerial types. Even if your boss doesn't fit the type exactly, you'll see enough of him or her that the descriptions will be familiar. More important, the advice about how to manage each type will be relevant.

Before explaining how this book evolved from my experiences and how the advice will impact your relationships with bosses and your career, I want to tell you a short story that illustrates why this book is so necessary now.

SAILING WITH THE BULLY

A number of years ago, I went sailing with my boss at the time, and it started out wonderfully. The sun was shining, the wind was steady, the sea was calm. Best of all, my manager was in a great mood, and we were having a great time talking about work issues as well as other matters. A few hours later, though, a front moved in and the sea became rough. As conditions deteriorated, he reverted to form. As a manager, he was a Bully type—tough, aggressive, decisive, used to giving orders and having them obeyed without question. Though he could be gracious and accommodating when it suited his purposes, his classic Bully traits would come to the surface whenever he was under significant stress. As the wind stretched the sails tight and the boat rose, fell, and tilted at a precarious angle, my boss ordered me to put my life jacket on. He snapped at me when I asked a question. He shouted at me to get something from the other end of the boat and told me, "Hurry up!"

I recognized that he was becoming the tough captain of the ship rather than my friend and colleague, and that he was responding in the only way he knew how to a difficult situation. Nonetheless, it wasn't a life-or-death situation but one that required him to take charge. An outside observer would have thought him rude and bad-tempered.

Fortunately, I understood this type of boss and was accustomed to this type of mood swing when he was under pressure. I understood that this wasn't a time to challenge or question him; I didn't take his rudeness personally. I followed orders, and as soon as we were safely back in port, he returned to his old charming self. He complimented me on how well I had done in a difficult situation, and I thanked him for helping us get back safely.

In many ways, we interacted the same way at work. I had learned how to handle him when he was being difficult. I knew when I could question his directions and when I could not. Because I grasped his Bully type, I was able to maintain a strong working relationship with him, and he in turn was supportive of my career aspirations in the company.

I don't want to make this sound easier than it was. It took time and study to figure out this managerial type. The Bully was complex, like all the types we'll discuss. He had good traits and bad ones, and it took a while to identify what made him tick and what ticked him off. But I had observed and worked for other Bullies in the past, and I was able to "get" him eventually. This made managing my manager infinitely easier than it would have been, especially when he was under stress.

Most bosses today work in highly stressful environments. I'm sure my sailing metaphor isn't lost on you—every manager is trying to navigate through stormy seas as companies and industries undergo significant change. To deal effectively with a boss under pressure, you need to know her well. I'm not saying you need to know her personality as much as her managerial persona. Certainly the two concepts are related; many people's best and worst qualities are muted when you're having lunch with them or interacting with them socially, but when they put on their boss hat and they're struggling to meet a tight deadline, they change. They exhibit certain traits that define them as bosses rather than as people.

I want to communicate the traits of each of the six types because I really could have used a book like this earlier in my career. Let me tell you about that career and how it catalyzed my interest in and study of boss types.

DEALING WITH BOSSES IN BELGIUM, FRANCE, THE UNITED STATES, AFRICA, SOUTH AMERICA, AND ELSEWHERE

I've had a diverse number of bosses and observed many more in action. If any book can be said to spring directly from experience, this one is it. I started out in France as an accountant and a lawyer, but after working as an attorney for a large accounting firm, I transitioned into human resources, first for a private company and then for Kraft Jacobs Suchard. Most of my work experience, though, has been with Philip Morris in various executive HR positions around the globe. At one point, I was a European vice president responsible for 15,000 employees. Now in a similar HR executive position with Bacardi, I have been involved in the recruitment, selection, downsizing, outplacement, training, and coaching processes for thousands of managers and leaders working all over the world. Because of my work, I know my bosses.

I know Bill, a leader in Europe who was smart, empathetic, and terrified of making a decision.

I know Rene, a former top official in the Communist party who was as tough and as myopic as his background implies.

I know Boris, a visionary who was constantly testing new theories as his people scrambled to get up to speed.

I know Lydia, a control freak who didn't let her direct reports issue a memo or send certain types of e-mails without her approval.

I know Emil, a boss who was skilled at getting promoted in large part because he was equally skilled at blaming others when things went wrong.

Working for these and other individuals could be inspiring one moment and frustrating seconds later. In some instances, I found myself learning a great deal from them, and in other instances, I found myself repeating the same tasks and learning nothing at all. There were occasions when I felt we enjoyed a synergistic relationship that was highly productive and satisfying, and there were other occasions when I felt like we were the equivalent of a dysfunctional married couple.

It occurred to me that if I could manage my manager, I could maximize the positive experiences and minimize the negative ones. This epiphany came to me relatively early in my career when I was working for an entrepreneurial organization and a boss who was tremendously aggressive and domineering. I would go to work and dread our encounters, knowing that he was likely to chew me out for some mistake or refuse to listen to what I had to say. One day, an organizational catastrophe took place. What was worse, my boss was responding to it in his usual manner: quickly, angrily, and without obtaining sufficient information and ideas from his people.

I told him I thought he was making a mistake. I suggested an alternative response that I thought would be more effective.

He wasn't happy with my disagreement, and he didn't do what I suggested. But from that moment on, he treated me differently. He listened more to what I had to say. He gave me more responsibility. He rarely became angry with me. Inadvertently, I had discovered that what he respected most were people who were willing to stand up to him. This was a counterintuitive behavior—it seemed that if you were to stand up to him, he'd cut you off at the knees. But it worked.

I realized that if you possessed a number of strategies for a number of different boss types, you could make your work life infinitely easier, more satisfying, and more productive. I began formulating those strategies and using them to my advantage in various work situations, and from these efforts, supplemented by discussions with other direct reports and bosses about my ideas, this book evolved.

WHAT YOU'LL FIND AND HOW TO USE IT

Let me give you a preview of what you'll find in the following pages and then suggest how you can implement the lessons learned.

The first six chapters describe the main six types of bosses. In each of these chapters, I'll talk about one "manager" I worked for who exemplified a type. I put manager in quotes because each boss I refer to as being mine is actually a composite of a few bosses I worked for or observed who represent a type. In this way, I can keep the identities of my bosses disguised.

You'll also find that each of the six types reflects the complexity of bosses. In other words, each type of boss has good points and bad ones; each type functions well or poorly in certain situations; and one type may be great for a direct report with a certain personality and terrible for another direct report who has a different style. What I've tried to do is reflect the reality of each common boss and not divide them into good bosses and bad bosses—which isn't to say that all these types are created equal. As you'll see, one of them is more difficult to work for than the others (at least for most people), and one of them is more fun.

I think it's fair to give you a snapshot of each type here, though with the proviso that this snapshot doesn't do their complexity justice. Still, I think it will be useful if you start thinking about these types before I go into detail about them:

- The Bully—aggressive, command-and-control type; can deliver great results, but can also take bad risks and be a tough person to work for.

- The Good—consistent, calm, communicative, but has problem with risk or anything that upsets the applecart.

- The Kaleidoscope—shifting persona focused on accumulating and consolidating power; extremely bright and business savvy, but also difficult to get to know the real person and easy to resent controlling personality.

- The Star—high-energy, dramatic, and action-oriented, but has little patience with red tape or anything that requires patience; impulsiveness can get the group in trouble.

- The Scientist—highly logical and reliant on a theory of the case, open to feedback, but also can stubbornly stick to a theory beyond all reason; can also be distracted and difficult to communicate with in this state.

- The Navel—big ego in need of constant feeding; this ego can drive group to decide and execute with speed and skill; can also drive people to distraction as this boss makes everything about him.

Each of these chapters will follow essentially the same format, providing you with information about each type, suggesting ways you can best deal with them from personal and professional perspectives, and offering a "secret strategy"—a simple but often unexpected approach for working with a boss.

After these six core chapters, you'll find one on managing these six types in specific situations: during crises, after a big win, when you're angling for a promotion, and arguing for taking a risk. Each type has a particular way of dealing with these events, and it's useful to know what that way is and how you can manage your boss situationally.

In Chapter 8, you'll learn about secondary boss types—ones that aren't as common as our main six but are still likely to cross your path during your career. I had a great deal of enjoyment writing this chapter, and I think you'll enjoy reading it—the types covered here tend to be a bit on the edge, and their actions and antics are entertaining. You'll learn about the Geek boss, the Con Artist, and others.

If I had to pick a favorite subject, though, it's the one discussed in the final chapter. Here I'll introduce the concept of the Seventh Leader. This is an ideal type of boss, one I hope all of you will aspire to. The Seventh Leader is someone who is brilliant at listening to and learning from his teams (among other qualities). While I've never encountered anyone who matched the model of a Seventh Leader, I have seen and worked for bosses who have the knack of both leading their teams and being led by them. This chapter will also suggest how you might look for and do everything possible to find jobs working for people who approach this ideal in their management style, and how to make the most of working for someone who exhibits Seventh Leader traits.

Even before you read the book's chapters, you may automatically have started comparing your boss to the ones I've just described. As you compared, you may have said to yourself, "My boss isn't exactly like any of the six you mentioned." This is possible. While some of you will have managers who are obviously one of the types, others of you will struggle to find an exact match.

Don't struggle. The purpose of creating these managerial types is ease of use in managing your boss. It would be a rather laborious process to describe the 1,001 types that may actually exist, and even more laborious to provide specific advice for managing each one. I've chosen these six because they are common types. This means that your current boss is likely to be closely related to one of them, even if he isn't a perfect match. Therefore, find the type that is most like your boss; you'll find that the advice is generally applicable despite differences.

More importantly, my goal is to help you starting thinking about how to manage your manager in a new way. The book provides a process for figuring out such things as identifying the key traits of your boss, thinking about how to deal with these traits from both a relationship and a productivity standpoint, figuring out if you're a good fit with this boss type, and having a strategy in reserve to help you make the most of the boss experience. This process will work with any type of boss, be it one of the six detailed, the additional ones discussed in Chapter 8, or any other type.

Too often, we respond to our bosses based on a single characteristic. If we have a Navel boss, for instance, we can't get past her huge ego and how irritating this quality is. Or if we have a Good boss, his boring consistency and unwillingness to take risks become the lens through which we see him. What I hope to convey is that we need to broaden our perspective on bosses. The Navel is more than his ego, and the Good is more than his consistency. Seeing these bosses in deeper terms provides us with more options for managing them effectively.

WHAT MAKES YOUR BOSS TICK?

If you can answer this question, you have a much better chance of managing your manager. Unfortunately, it's more difficult than ever before to answer the question accurately for a number of reasons.

First, we often don't stay with one boss long enough to figure him out. The turnover in organizations is so high that either your boss leaves or you do before you've had the time to get to know him well. You can't size up your boss in one or two or even three meetings. It takes a series of interactions in a variety of situations before you can start determining your boss's makeup. If you boss is around for only six months, by the time you start getting a handle on who she is, she's gone.

Second, increased travel and flexible work schedules often make it difficult to get to know a boss, even one who is there for a sustained period of time. You may be on the road a lot, as is your boss, so your face-to-face interactions are infrequent. Similarly, you may be working out of your home while he's in the office (or vice versa); you may be located in two different offices; or you may be working different schedules.

Third, so much of our communication with our colleagues these days is via electronics—phones, e-mails, teleconferences, text messaging, and so on. If this is the main way you get to know your boss, you probably don't know him well at all.

Fourth, you may be splitting your time between two or more bosses. For instance, you're a member of a functional group with one boss and a member of a cross-functional team with another boss. This dilutes time spent with a single boss and makes it harder to figure her out.

Given all this, you need to ask yourself a series of questions about your boss to figure out what makes her tick. While the book will prompt you to ask very specific questions about your boss, the following more general ones will get you thinking in a "ticking" frame of mind and get you accustomed to going beyond the routine surface questions we usually ask about our bosses:

- What single behavior or attitude is most likely to upset your boss?

- When is your boss most pleased with direct reports? What do they say or do during the course of carrying out assignments or in meetings that earns his approval?

- What are your boss's demons? What work issue do you think keeps him up at night pacing the floor?

- What do you think your manager's career objectives are? What capstone position is he aiming for? What does he need to accomplish to achieve these objectives?

- What drives your manager? What noncareer motivators push her? Is she after power, money, fame, security, knowledge, innovation, etc.?

- What trait or attitude that you possess makes you think you are well-suited to work for this particular boss? What trait or attitudes makes you think you are ill-suited?

- If your boss were a famous movie star, politician, or other celebrity, who would he be? What particular traits does he share in common with this well-known individual?

This is not a definitive list of questions by any means. In fact, you probably can (and should) create some of your own. But they're offered to help you start digging down and identifying who your boss is at her core. Don't be satisfied to define her simply or based on office rumor. Use your own experiences to form a conclusion about the drivers and demons of your boss. By doing so, you'll be well prepared to use the more specific advice that follows.

THE BENEFITS: WHY INVEST IN KNOWING YOUR BOSS (AND READING THIS BOOK)

Some people deal with a difficult boss relationship by gritting their teeth and toughing it out. They are unhappy in the relationship, not learning much and not doing their best work, but they hang in there for a variety of reasons—they hope their boss will retire soon or that they'll get another job. Other people have okay relationships with their boss and accept that they're not getting as much as they might from the situation but rationalize that it's better than working for the jerk who used to be their boss.

As I noted earlier, I believe that just about every boss can be managed. What that means is that people can be proactive in working with their managers; they don't just have to sit there and *be managed*. Passively accepting an unacceptable situation or tolerating a boss who isn't doing a lot for you strikes me as unnecessary.

In my many years as both a boss and a direct report, I have seen how people make bad boss situations into good ones and good ones into great ones. They do it by taking charge of managing the relationship, resulting in three types of benefits:

- **Facilitating the day-to-day personal interactions between you and your boss.** Is there a lot of tension between you and your boss that makes you uncomfortable? Do you find it difficult to talk to your manager or does she find it difficult to talk to you? Do you find that when you do talk, there's a lot of miscommunication? If you don't get along with your boss, it's a miserable experience. You don't need to be best friends, but you do need to establish a mutually acceptable working relationship. By using the suggestions you'll find on how to manage your boss, the relationship should benefit greatly.

- **Helping you help your boss be more effective.** Many direct reports know what their boss is doing wrong but don't know how to communicate it without negative repercussions. Or they have ideas they believe would help their boss run the group even more effectively than he does, but they are uncertain about how to propose these ideas without causing their boss to respond defensively or angrily. Another benefit of this book is that it will give you tactics to make your boss a more effective manager and the group more productive.

- **Giving you tools to increase your work quality in the short term and boost your career in the long term.** Knowing how to work with your boss with greater efficiency and effectiveness can result in many short-term gains—you'll receive more challenging assignments and ones that take better advantage of your talents. In the long run, the tools included here will help your boss better appreciate your contributions and rely on them more. Your achievements will be noted by your manager (and by others in the organization), who should be favorably disposed to reward you with raises, promotions, and so on.

All these benefits don't happen immediately. It's unlikely that when you finish this book and put its lessons into practice, you'll be transformed suddenly from a C player to an A player in the organization. As they say, all good things take time. But time becomes your friend rather than your enemy. When you become proficient at managing your boss, you develop an ally in your quest to do your job to the best of your ability and in your attempt to achieve career objectives.

With all this as preamble, it's time to examine our first boss type, a type who appears tough but is not as difficult to manage as he appears: the Bully.

MANAGING
YOUR
MANAGER

THE BULLY

Limit the Pain,
Target the Gain

My Bully looked like his moniker, in that he was a big guy. The Bully, however, doesn't have to be physically large to be intimidating. I've known Bullies who are small in stature yet have a swagger and sneer about them that inspire fear. There are women Bullies as well as men. And the Bully may be a first-time manager or the CEO.

In short, this type comes in all shapes and sizes.

The word *bully* connotes a number of negative traits, but like all boss archetypes that I'll discuss, this one is a mixture of positives and negatives. In fact, the positives are often the flip side of the negatives—you don't get one without the other.

Let's look at my particular Bully, and then we'll examine the best way of managing this heavy-handed heavy hitter.

THE BULLY IN ACTION

As some researchers demonstrate, the three critical factors for the making of a CEO are self-esteem, self-confidence, and self-control. My Bully lacked this last one, a common failing among Bully bosses. These managers have unexpected bursts of anger, and their volatility contributes to their intimidating presence. It's one thing when a boss becomes angry over a costly mistake, but it's something else entirely when his rage seems to come out of nowhere.

My Bully hated surprises. He was most likely to fly off the handle and castigate people when he was unprepared for what he saw or heard. For instance, Joshua, the Bully's direct report, once made a presentation to the Bully's boss at which our entire group was present. Joshua did an excellent job, but during the presentation he revealed that we had made a second trip to a key customer to correct a complaint. It was a relatively innocuous admission, but the Bully didn't think so. After the meeting, behind closed doors, the Bully's screams echoed down the hallway, and Joshua slunk out of his office like a whipped dog. In fact, Joshua was so shaken by the encounter that he tried to avoid the Bully whenever possible, and his effectiveness diminished considerably; he left the company within the year.

The Bully was intensely competitive, so when another group within the company delivered better results than our group, or an outside competitor did well, he erupted. Sometimes his eruptions had a touch of paranoia to them. He was convinced that there were leaks—that someone in our group had revealed something to another group that gave them an edge. Or he believed that we had been careless with our electronic correspondence, allowing competitors to observe what projects we were working on and take advantage of this knowledge. Rather than accepting that there were other good teams and companies out there, the Bully would browbeat us as a group as well as individually for our failings. Like most Bullies, he was skilled at knowing where

THE BULLY

3

an employee's most vulnerable spot was and hitting it with a barbed comment. Judy, who had been fired early on in her career for taking a risk that resulted in her company losing a significant amount of money, tended to play it safe with her decisions. The Bully, fully aware of her past problems, would needle her unmercifully: "Judy, is this really what you want to do, or what your fear of failure is telling you to do?"

At times, the Bully micromanaged when he should have supervised and delegated. Even worse, he let you know that he was taking over your task because you weren't smart enough, fast enough, or savvy enough to complete it effectively. He thought nothing of taking back an assignment he had given you and doing it himself. While he often was very good at executing these tasks, his micromanaging not only was demeaning, but it prevented learning and growth; it also made people wary of taking on stretch assignments where there was a good chance of making mistakes.

The Bully, though, possessed the strengths of his type as well as the weaknesses. He was highly aggressive, competitive, and driven, and this often resulted in our group meeting or exceeding our objectives. He was not intimidated by anyone, and he was willing to stand in front of the company's top executives and defend our group with convincing ardor. New or unfamiliar situations were not a problem for him as they are for some executives. At one point, our group faced a crisis about which the Bully knew very little, yet he took it on with great confidence and handled it with great effectiveness. Confidence to the point of arrogance has its benefits.

Despite his temper and intimidating demeanor, many good people wanted to work for the Bully. This was due, in large part, to the Bully's reputation for securing top bonuses and rewarding his favorites—if you were on his good side, he made organizational life easy for you. He also created excitement and energy around his teams, much as motivational sports coaches do. He pushed hard, posed challenges, created pragmatic strategies, and rewarded performance.

The people who got along best with the Bully tended to be either jaded or highly ambitious. Members of the latter group felt that he could help advance their careers—if the Bully could get them the compensation and promotions they wanted, he could yell as much as he wanted. The jaded group felt that the Bully was savvy about office politics and would use the force of his personality to protect those he liked; they figured he offered them more protection in tough times than managers who were nice but ineffectual.

The people who had problems with him harbored more idealistic notions of what business could and should be. Up until the time I began working for the Bully, I had subscribed to certain beliefs about being a manager in an organization. Perhaps naively, I had always assumed managers joined and stayed with an organization because they believed in what the company stood for. They possessed a purpose that transcended their personal mission. They were loyal to the company, their bosses, and their teams. Though they certainly had individual goals—in terms of salary, bonuses, titles, and so on—they were also motivated by factors larger than these personal objectives. While my previous bosses had flaws, most were driven by a group vision—they wanted their teams, their departments, their divisions, and their organizations to do well.

The Bully wanted himself to do well, and if others also did well, that was fine but of secondary concern. Such selfish behavior was difficult to deal with. At best, it was disillusioning. At worst, it bred cynicism and similarly selfish behaviors. The Bully demonstrated his me-first attitude in many ways, but the most egregious usually had to do with his compensation. On at least one occasion, he manipulated the numbers to ensure that he would receive the highest bonus allowed, justifying his behaviors by saying that he "deserved it." Similarly, he made it clear to his team that they were receiving their bonuses because of his heroic efforts and not because they deserved them. He tried to bully them into believing that but for the grace of him, there would be no good bonuses.

To call him Machiavellian would be an oversimplification, but he certainly was manipulative. On his best days, he manipulated in ways that helped our group achieve highly ambitious objectives and contributed to the company's overall success. On his worst days, he manipulated out of spite, anger, or just because it was in his nature.

TELLING TRAITS

Many managers can lose their tempers and be intimidating at times, but they are not necessarily Bullies. What distinguishes the Bully from other types is that he is consistently intimidating, pushing other people around, losing control, driving toward results, displaying incredible confidence, and being selfish. Use the following questions to determine if your manager's modus operandi is that of a Bully:

- Does she try to get you to carry out assignments or meet goals through fear and intimidation?
- Is your manager constantly berating you in order to make herself look good by comparison?

- Does she consistently deliver good results, in large part through her aggressiveness, drive, and toughness?

- Does she tend to attract ambitious cynics, while value-driven people and sensitive souls struggle to work for her?

- Is she willing to be tough with her own bosses as well as her direct reports?

- Are her ultimate motives selfish? (i.e., Is she much more concerned with her own performance than with how well the team, department, or division does?)

- Do her self-confidence and bluster allow her to handle crises and unfamiliar situations better than most managers?

Perhaps an even more telling identification factor involves the paradoxical persona the Bully creates. Contrary to the images usually conjured by this term, the Bully isn't a one-dimensional tyrant (though tyranny is definitely part of his repertoire). Instead, the Bully tends to generate fear, respect, and fascination in equal measures. The fear can derive from many sources, from obvious belligerence to more subtle demonstrations of power. My Bully, for instance, used a combination of straight talk (telling you what he thought, even if it was hurtful) and a commanding presence to intimidate; even when he wasn't yelling or threatening, he inspired a certain amount of fear.

Respect came from his willingness to say what he thought, even when he was talking to his own bosses. The Bully often gets what he wants, and his ability to get what his people need in the bargain creates at least grudging respect. Just as we admire coaches like Bob Knight who display appalling behaviors but get results, we admire bosses who produce consistently.

Fascination is a result of the Bully being a complex character. When I joined the Bully's group, the first thing he asked me was nothing that any boss had ever asked me before. He wasn't curious about what I hoped to learn or how I might contribute to the group. Instead, the first question out of his mouth was, "Did they give you more money ["they" being these Guys in the Headquarters]?" The Bully frequently says and does things no one else would say or do. The Bully is always the object of his people's speculations: Why is he so driven? Why does he feel compelled to insult everyone? What makes him so angry?

Therefore, if you're trying to determine if your boss is a Bully, think about whether he evokes fear, respect, and fascination much more so than other bosses. This trio of responses is a good sign that you're working for a Bully.

Finally, make the distinction between a permanent and a temporary Bully. Some bosses like to test people when they first join the group or when the Bully first becomes their manager. Their method is to subject a given individual to intense questioning and criticism, to give them stretch assignments to see how they handle it. They may not even do it consciously—they are anxious and want to communicate to their people that they are not pushovers—but the net effect is off-putting. These bosses, however, are involved in temporary testing. After a few weeks or a month or two at most, they ease up. They may act like the typical Bully boss, but they're only acting. They will revert to their natural type after this break-in period.

A real Bully, on the other hand, continues to be intimidating and bitingly critical indefinitely.

INTERPERSONAL TACTICS: HOW TO DEAL WITH THE ANGER, INTIMIDATION, AND OTHER TRAITS

The Bully can be a challenging manager to manage, especially if you're not used to dealing with this type. If you've never worked for a Bully before, it may seem as if she has a personal vendetta against you or as if there's nothing you can do to please her. You may find yourself reacting defensively to her derisive critiques of your work, which only makes a bad situation worse.

Before suggesting what you can do to handle the negative emotional reactions that come with working for a Bully, consider how two other people dealt with this situation.

Vince was the creative director of a large ad agency, and he had enjoyed a stellar career, winning awards for commercials he and his teams had helped create and demonstrating great skill as a presenter to agency clients and prospects. Vince had two relatively young and inexperienced copywriters in his group—Dennis and Sheila. As was his habit, he picked on them mercilessly. When they presented concepts to him, he often shot them down with thick sarcasm. Once, he told Dennis that the idea for a print ad he came up was worthy of a five-year-old. After Sheila had worked for over a week on a radio commercial for one of the agency's largest clients, he told her that if they presented it, the client would fire them and be justified in doing so. Vince often used a line with them that he had used many times before with young copywriters and art directors: "Maybe you should consider a career in accounting, since that field requires little creativity."

Dennis was devastated by Vince's bullying tactics. On his ride home from work, he would think about all the mean things Vince had said to him, running them through his mind over and over, trying to determine if he was as untalented as Vince implied he was. He talked to his girlfriend incessantly about Vince, and she quickly grew tired of his obsession with his boss; she eventually forbade Dennis from even mentioning Vince's name. At work, Dennis became so anxious about Vince's reactions that his work pace slowed—he tried to think of every objection Vince might have to his ads, and he thought of so many that he had trouble finalizing anything. He reached a point where he hated coming to work and made a conscious effort to avoid personal contact with Vince, using e-mail and phone to communicate with him whenever possible. Finally, he quit his job, deciding that he could no longer tolerate working for a Bully.

Sheila, on the other hand, wasn't particularly bothered by Vince after she adjusted to his style. At first, she had reacted in a similar way to Dennis; she had never had a boss treat her so rudely. After a while, though, she realized that despite being a jerk, he was a very smart, accomplished jerk who could teach her a lot about advertising and help her career. She learned that the best way to deal with Vince's bullying manner was to adopt the stance of a novice (even though she had been in the business for three years) and try to find the learning buried in Vince's invective. When he told her once that an ad she and her art director had produced was likely to send potential customers running to a competitor's brand, she asked him why he thought that was likely. He answered her, and though his answer was typically sarcastic, it contained wisdom that she was able to use.

Similarly, Sheila recognized that she needed to develop a thick skin if she were to continue to work for and learn from Vince. This was easier said than done, but it helped Sheila to talk to others who had been in Vince's group for a few years and assured her that though he was never a particularly nice boss, he was great at presenting his people's work and selling it to clients, all which advanced their careers. Sheila was motivated to develop a thick skin, and, after a few months, she was able to handle the way he browbeat her when he felt her effort was sub-par. Sheila said it was almost a "Zen-like" approach, how she filtered out the meanness in his tone and words and focused exclusively on his insight into what did and did not make a good ad.

Within two years, Sheila was promoted to group copy supervisor, and a year later she became an associate creative director. Even then, Vince continued to berate her (though not as frequently or as nastily), but she also knew that he valued her and told herself that "it was just his way."

The moral of this story isn't that Sheila's approach is always the right approach. Some people find Bullies impossible to work for, and quitting may be a better option than to go to work each day and develop an ulcer. You have to know yourself and recognize which boss type is particularly difficult for you to deal with, given your psychological makeup (more about that at the end of the chapter).

Still, the following advice is valid for most people and will help them manage the Bully by managing their own personal responses to this type.

Don't Take It Personally

This is the equivalent of Sheila's tactic of developing a thick skin. Try to see things from the Bully's point of view. It may be that he sees his overly critical approach as the best way to help people learn and avoid career-killing mistakes. It's possible that he's so focused on helping his group meet highly ambitious objectives—objectives he is driven to meet—that he is intolerant of any misstep that hampers achieving these goals. In other words, if you can see the "logic" behind the Bully's yelling and hostility, then you may be able to take the personal edge off of it.

Once, when we had a large company meeting in which my Bully was answering general questions for employees, he introduced our team in a relatively pleasant manner. The only problem was that he forgot to introduce one member of the team—the HR person, who happened to be me. After the meeting, I heard another executive mention to the Bully that he had neglected to introduce me. The Bully said, "Yes, you're right, I forgot to mention the HR guy, a necessary evil."

When you hear something like this, your impulse is to cry or scream. Instead, what you do is tell yourself that you're not going to let him get to you and that his style is to pick on everyone, not just you.

Find the Humor

Admittedly, there's nothing funny about getting pushed around and yelled at by your boss. In fact, it's humiliating. Yet if you think about it, there's something absurd about a grown man who feels he has to act like the toughest kid in the schoolyard. Bullies are made to be mocked. They are ridiculous actors, puffing themselves up and pushing others around just because they are in a position to do so. Laughing at them privately can take the edge off the hurt you feel. It can turn the tables on the Bully's strategy; in your mind, he's the object of your derision.

If the above approach doesn't suffice, use humor to deflect your manager's aggression. Try acting the fool: "How could I have been so stupid to go over budget on the project? A smart organization would just take me out back and shoot me." Some Bully bosses will laugh or at least see the absurdity in the situation and stop attacking, at least for the moment. While some Bullies are notorious for lacking a sense of humor, they still might back off when they realize their bullying isn't having the desired effect: to turn you into a quivering blob. Think of the school bully who taunts only because he wants to see you turn red or cry; if you respond with humor, he's not getting what he's after.

LIMIT THE PAIN, TARGET THE GAIN

In other words, recognize that working for the Bully is a temporary assignment and that you can set limits on how long you'll tolerate it; determine that within the time frame you set, you'll use this assignment to build your competencies so you are a more effective and marketable professional.

Psychologically, setting limits and specifying goals makes difficult situations more tolerable. The Bully may be unpleasant to work for in certain respects, but when you know you only have to deal with him for one year, it ceases to be such an onerous assignment. In the same way, if you figure out what you need to get out of the job to help your career, you have a positive incentive for serving out the term you set. Perhaps you need to gain global experience and working for the Bully will help you get it. Remember, too, that the Bully tends to be pragmatic and effective. Working on his team may provide you with a good track record to obtain other jobs, whether in your own company or elsewhere. It may also result in bonuses and promotions, which are worthwhile gains in and of themselves.

PROFESSIONAL TACTICS: HOW TO WORK EFFECTIVELY FOR A BULLY

Any manager can be managed, even a Bully who belittles and screams as routinely as other managers encourage and provide constructive criticism. They must be managed, however, with a keen understanding of what unleashes their inner Bully and what placates or pleases it. Based on my experiences with my Bully as well as conversations with other business people who have worked for this managerial type, here are the optimum ways of working with this boss:

AVOID SURPRISES

Bullies hate to be blindsided. Nothing would enrage my Bully more than having other people—especially bosses or customers—know something before he did. If you'll recall our earlier example, the Bully was furious with Joshua when he made a presentation and disclosed a bit of information the Bully was unaware of.

Therefore, keep Bullies informed of significant and even relatively insignificant developments. Though it's difficult to tell bad news to Bullies because of their tempers, it's better than them finding out the bad news later from some other source. Bullies respect people who talk straight and keep them in the loop. They might not like what you tell them, but you'll avoid their fury when they find something out that they feel you should have told them.

BE A SOURCE FOR NEWS

This follows from the earlier "keep them in the loop" advice. Bullies relish feeling like they are plugged in to what is happening in the organization. They crave control and power, and feeding them tidbits of information satisfies this craving. More to the point, it makes you seem like an insider to the Bully. In fact, Bullies tend to prefer receiving information from secondhand sources, believing it has greater value than a direct statement.

For instance, one member of our team, Peter, was a very talented guy who was becoming increasingly unhappy with his limited responsibility as well as his compensation. Like many people, he wasn't about to complain to the Bully, fearing his wrath. As the HR head, I felt it was my job to help our group keep valuable employees, so I told the Bully that Peter was dissatisfied and had been contacted by a headhunter. I suggested that he might want to talk to him and do whatever was necessary to keep him. The Bully was grateful for this knowledge (though of course he didn't express that gratitude), since he valued people who could help our group deliver results, and Peter was one of those people. Shortly thereafter, Peter was promoted.

If you can earn the trust of other members of your group and be the one who communicates their problems and requirements to the Bully, you can elevate your status in the Bully's eyes. Admittedly, this can be an intimidating "job," since it means having to tell the Bully things he might not want to hear and listen to him rant and rave. The tradeoff of elevated status, though, is worth it.

DEVELOP A PROFITABLE AREA OF EXPERTISE

Figure out what your group's knowledge or skill deficit is and make it your business to become the go-to person when issues arise in this area. Focus on the obstacles to meeting your numbers or achieving objectives. Does your team require someone who is skilled in social networking? Do you need someone who has great research abilities? Are you short an expert in global marketing? Do you need someone who can scrounge resources when they are in short supply?

Whatever it is, becoming an expert in this area will make the Bully far more generous toward you than he might otherwise be. For instance, I became our group's expert in pensions, compensation, and other financial issues. The Bully was obsessed with these issues, convinced that we needed to lobby for a better deal from management in all these areas. The Bully needed someone who could communicate knowledgeably about these matters with management, and when I became that person, his harsh attitude toward me softened considerably.

In fact, the Bully encouraged me to take courses and capitalize on other training opportunities in these financial areas. While he wasn't a big fan of training—he was highly derogatory in his attitude to trainers and their roles in corporations—he was willing to support people who sought training in areas that directly benefited him and helped the group deliver its numbers.

Build Alliances That Help Get Things Done

As more and more companies switch to a matrix structure or restructure in other ways that create the same reporting ambiguity, Bullies struggle. They typically have command-and-control mentalities and prefer the traditional pyramid to all other structures. They find it frustrating when it's unclear who someone is supposed to report to, the line person in a local market or the staff person many miles away.

Relationship-building is a skill Bullies often lack, and if you can master this skill and navigate the ambiguity that defines many structures, you will be in a much better position to execute. To get things done, you need to establish connections with both line and staff people and figure out a way to meet both their needs.

Lena, for instance, worked for the head of manufacturing at a mid-sized automotive aftermarket products company. Tony, an ex-military man, had come up through the engineering ranks and had a drill sergeant mentality. Lena, an MBA from a top school, had almost nothing in common with Tony, who inherited Lena when he took over the function. Tony found Lena to be lacking in technological experience and expertise, and he also disliked how she emphasized growth and development of people. To Tony, the best people were the best engineers, and the others were a necessary evil. As the company profits fell during the recession, they brought in a new CEO who flattened the structure and emphasized cross-functional teams over traditional functional groups. Tony floundered in this new environment, finding that he could no longer intimidate people into doing his bidding. Lena, however, was a great networker, and she used this ability to help Tony forge alliances with individuals in HR, marketing, and finance that he had formerly ignored or been brusque with. These alliances made it possible for Tony to implement programs and plans that had been stalled, and his gratitude to Lena was such that he made her his second-in-command.

THE DON'TS: WHAT DOESN'T WORK WITH BULLIES

More so than most managerial types, Bullies have certain behaviors and attitudes that they despise. If you're aware of what they are, they're easy to avoid. Unfortunately, they're not obvious don'ts. In fact, they might seem counterintuitive at first. Still, just knowing what these red flags are can prevent you from committing blunders that will make it difficult if not impossible to manage your boss.

DON'T BE A "YES" MAN OR WOMAN

Some people believe that the best way to deal with a Bully is to tell him what he wants to hear and do exactly what he says he wants done. This is a huge mistake. Some Bullies may say they want you to follow their orders to the letter or give the impression that they don't want any debate or questions, but that's just their egos talking. What they really want is someone who can help them accomplish their objectives. Bullies are pragmatists; they subscribe to the principle that *la fin justifie les moyens* (the ends justifies the means). Therefore, they might not like being challenged, but they will accept it and learn to appreciate it if it creates improved results.

Use this suggestion judiciously. If you're always telling the Bully no or questioning his decisions, he'll probably try and get rid of you. Pick your spots. Wait until you're convinced your manager is making a huge mistake or until you come up with an idea you truly believe in. *At that point, make your case.* This last sentence is italicized for a reason. It's not enough just to challenge an idea or question a decision. You have to make a convincing argument by doing the following:

- Rehearse the logic of your argument before making it; make sure you know what you want to say and that you're saying it clearly and rationally.

- Make your point concisely. Bullies are impatient by nature, and if you're long-winded, you'll lose the Bully's attention.

- Emphasize the positive outcome. Focus the Bully's attention on what he (or the group) will get out of doing as you suggest.

DO THE TASKS HE HATES OR ISN'T GOOD AT

In general, Bullies hate and aren't good at soft skills. They're not active listeners; they don't enjoy extended debate and discussion; they have difficulty using finesse and subtlety to obtain what they need from someone; they aren't adept at dealing with any type of people problems.

Recognizing where your Bully comes up short and how you help him compensate won't earn you any thanks from this manager. In fact, he may resent that you can do something he cannot. At the same time, he'll also understand the invaluable service you're performing. Few Bullies have so much power and influence that they can ignore their weaknesses. Sooner or later, these failings will impact their results, and that's one thing Bullies can't stomach.

I used to handle union negotiations for my Bully. As you might expect, the give-and-take, the seemingly endless debates over relatively small matters, the need to accept another person's point of view—all this drove him insane. So I handled it for him, and though he never admitted his lack of skill in this area or expressed much gratitude for my assistance, I know he depended on my ability to negotiate and called upon it frequently.

DELIVER MEASURABLE, MEANINGFUL RESULTS

Some managers value people for intangible but significant contributions—their creativity, their communication skills, their commitment and energy. The Bully doesn't care about these things. What matters to him is someone who produces, who completes tasks in ways that make the group and the boss look good.

Sheri worked for George, a major Bully at a high-powered consulting firm, and she had been hired (not by the Bully) in part for diversity reasons. Unlike many of the other young consultants, she lacked the right pedigree—top marks from an elite MBA program. At first, George treated Sheri like a pledge at a backward fraternity, subjecting her to the worst sort of hazing. He belittled her education at a state university; he nitpicked her reports, acting as if a typo were a sign of her overall incompetence. Once, during a meeting of their entire consulting team, he took a report she submitted and tore it to shreds, throwing the pieces in the air and screaming, "The mere existence of this report is an affront to every consultant at this firm."

Sheri didn't know what to do, but serendipity played a part in helping her learn how to manage her manager. They had a client meeting scheduled in Chicago, and George flew in from New York while one of his team members was supposed to fly in from Denver, where he was meeting with another client. Weather prevented his plane from taking off early that morning, and it was clear he wouldn't be able to get there in time. George had no choice but to ask Sheri to accompany him since no one else was available to attend. He limited her participation in the meeting to summarizing a few studies and detailing a few trends.

During the meeting, however, things weren't going well. The client was upset about a strategic blunder that they claimed the firm had contributed to. George, as usual, dismissed this assertion and proclaimed that the firm had placed the client on the right strategic course. Things became heated between them, and that's when Sheri stepped in. It wasn't anything she said but how she said it. Sheri was a warm, empathetic communicator, and the client responded immediately to her. He said she really seemed to understand what his company was going through, and at the end of the meeting, he told George that he would forgive the strategic blunder as long as Sheri took a bigger role in client service for the company.

George of course was furious initially. But he also recognized that Sheri had delivered a result that would make him look good. As he saw how Sheri could cement client relationships with her emotional intelligence, he backed off his hazing and gave her more responsibility.

CAN YOU MANAGE THIS BOSS TYPE? ASSESS YOUR OWN TOLERANCE

Ultimately, you need to determine if your boss is manageable. Please don't misunderstand. The premise of this book is that every manager is manageable if you know how to do it. The problem with this premise is that you might not want to do it. In other words, you may find yourself working for someone whose personality, style, and approach to work drive you up the wall. Therefore, determining your own tolerance for the particular manager you have is essential. The odds are that you'll find most of the types tolerable, but it may be that one of them is just too difficult for you to handle.

Certain traits are likely to make it extremely difficult to work for a Bully. Determine how many of the following traits apply to you. Are you someone who

- Hates to be criticized and can't deal with constant nitpicking and second guessing?

- Believes in civility and finds boorish, ill-tempered people impossible to communicate with?

- Has a strong fight-or-flight reflex when confronted by aggressive people and wants to smack them in the face or get as far from them as possible?

- Values learning and growth above all else and wants a mentor who will impart wisdom and skills consistently and kindly?

- Breaks down in tears or inwardly sobs when someone demeans you verbally and can't sleep at night after these incidents, replaying them constantly?

- Has been picked on since childhood, singled out for punishment by mean kids, harsh teachers, and others?

It's likely that you'll make at least one check mark next to a trait. If you possess only one or two traits, you probably can handle a Bully (though he may aggravate you more than others). If, however, you made three or more check marks, you should seriously question whether you want to work for a Bully.

THE SECRET STRATEGY

I'm going to end each of these chapters with a "secret" about the managerial type, something that isn't obvious but can be used as part of a strategy to manage a manager. Here's the Bully's secret:

A vulnerability to people who are self-controlled, flexible, and subtle.

The Bully is a brutal boxer who understands direct force. When someone comes at him from an odd angle, who uses judo instead of brawling, the Bully is flummoxed. My Bully could handle most people in our large organization no matter what their position or their power was, but he had great difficulty with those few individuals who he didn't get because their style was the opposite of his. At one point, a new, highly skilled person was brought in to work on the Bully's team. Almost immediately, the Bully began to confront him and question his expertise. Rather than react with anger or fear, this new person remained calm. Nothing the Bully said or did could get a rise out of him. In addition, he varied his style depending on the situation. One day he might respond to the Bully with a series of questions. The next day, he might offer a variety of options. The third day, he might say that he didn't know the answer. This new team member also was very clever about not being pinned down by the Bully. When the Bully would demand answers, solutions, and definitive actions, this new person would offer possibilities and what-if scenarios. They allowed the Bully to choose the right course of action without feeling like he had been instructed to do something. As a result, the Bully was wary of him and was a different person when he was around. He became far more thoughtful and less assertive than was his norm.

Therefore, if you find yourself struggling with how to act when you're in contact with the Bully, consider using this secret to moderate the Bully's worst tendencies. More specifically, try the following:

- Maintain your cool no matter what; don't let her see you sweat, scream, cry, or react in anything other than a calm manner.

- Adapt your behavior to the situation; demonstrate that you're a risk taker at times and that you're cautious at others; don't let her pin a label on you.

- Imply, infer, suggest, and ask questions when you communicate with the Bully; respond directly when she demands a direct response, but at other times, use nuanced communication.

Every manager has a secret vulnerability, and though you may not need to exploit it to manage the Bully, it's just one more tool you possess to keep the relationship viable for both of you.

THE GOOD

*Coping with
the Boredom*

he Good is good in many senses of that word. He's good at his job. He's good as his word. He delivers good results. He is also the epitome of managerial competence. Efficient is his middle name. If all this seems like I'm damning him with faint praise, that's not my purpose. Rather, recognize that if you have a Good boss, you don't have a Great one. You will be working for someone who is considerate, reasonable, logical, and knowledgeable, but you won't be working for someone who helps the group hit home runs or provides inspiring leadership.

After working for a boss like the Bully, of course, many people long for a Good boss. They've had it with egotistical behaviors and temper tantrums. They want stability and predictability, and a Good manager is eminently stable and predictable.

At the same time, working for a Good boss for any length of time may make you wish for a manager who takes risks, is spontaneous, and has a cutting edge aspect. In short, you may become bored or at least feel like things are too comfortable and slow-moving. You want to feel like you're in the middle of the action and instead it seems like you're on the periphery.

Circumstance, therefore, has a significant impact on how much you appreciate working for the Good. So too does your personality; some people find it easier to manage a predictable, competent boss than a volatile, highly effective one.

When I worked for the Good, I found it satisfying at times and stultifying at others. I also discovered techniques to increase the satisfaction and advance my career as well as approaches that made it less stultifying. I'll share those with you, but first I want to give you a more complete portrait of the Good boss.

THE GOOD IN ACTION

A Good manager isn't a 24/7 manager. Far from it. My Good boss separated his personal and professional lives, so you could go out for a meal with him and be assured it wouldn't be all business talk. Many managers bring their work home in one way or another; they work on assignments during the weekends or toss and turn at night as they contemplate a work problem. The Good rarely suffered from these homework issues. By focusing on business issues when he was in the office and then leaving them there until the next day, he could rejuvenate himself at night, on weekends, or on vacations. Unlike most of our colleagues, he usually turned off his BlackBerry during nonwork hours and didn't regularly check his e-mail at home or on vacation.

While some other managerial types practice this personal-professional separation, the Good liked it because it was sensible. The Good almost always did what made sense. He was not a manic or neurotic manager. Working for him was relatively easy, since I knew what he expected from me and what I could expect from him. The Good, unlike the Bully, didn't cause ulcers in his people. He ran groups where people generally felt comfortable and protected.

At the same time, I can't recall the Good ever doing or saying anything that was out of the box. As smart as the Good was, as consistent in his ability to deliver decent results, he never threw caution to the winds and suggested an approach where his belief in it trumped the logic of it. In other words, he didn't operate with his gut but with his head. It is impossible to imagine the Good pacing his home in the wee hours struggling to perfect his precedent-setting plan or delivering a rousing speech to generate support for it. It's much easier to picture him sleeping soundly or speaking logically.

One of the best things about working for this Good boss was that he was extraordinarily reasonable. Once, I suggested that taking acting classes would be a great way to facilitate development, that role-playing exercises and other acting techniques could help employees develop empathy, learn to be better speakers, and so on. As you might have guessed, the notion of having employees take acting classes was far too radical for the Good to endorse. At the same time, he listened to my arguments and told me that he would be happy to support me in my efforts to enroll in these classes. He saw that I really wanted to take them, that I marshaled a good argument in their favor, and he granted me permission to do so.

The Good disliked confrontation. When he joined the company, he inherited a direct report whose behavior and performance were representative of a previous regime. In a number of instances, she said or did things that reflected poorly on the Good. When people in his group pointed out that this direct report was causing him problems (the Good was either oblivious to them or deliberately ignoring them), he eventually conceded that this person had to go. But he was unwilling to do it directly. Instead, I had to handle it for him.

In another situation, a woman who worked in the Good's group complained that she was being sexually harassed by her boss. She made a compelling case that this harassment was taking place, and her boss had a reputation for this type of behavior. At the very least, the Good should have confronted him and issued an ultimatum that such behavior must cease immediately. Instead, he told this woman that it would be difficult to make the case against him and that she should warn him not to do it again. In this instance, not only did the Good want to avoid the emotional messiness of dealing with the man directly, but he wanted to avoid losing him (he was a key contributor to the group).

The Good shone in situations where everyone else was losing his head. I always marveled at his self-control. At one point, political maneuvering resulted in his responsibilities being diminished, despite his group's solid performance. Other managers might have quit in frustration or vented loudly to anyone who would listen. The Good, though, did nothing of the kind. While he confided in me that he was disappointed, he didn't rant and rave. This manager had great faith in the system. He viewed the event as a temporary setback and assumed that wrongs would eventually be righted. His willingness to stay the course and be loyal to an organization were commendable traits. He believed in the organization, and this belief conferred upon him a steadiness that impressed others.

Working for a Good manager is generally a satisfying experience. Despite his aversion to risk and his failure to innovate and motivate, he creates a relatively safe environment within a corporate culture where people can do good work. Management loves him because they can give him a task and be reasonably confident that he won't mess it up. They see him as a solid citizen who delivers consistent results. For these reasons, management tends to leave his groups alone. As frustrating as it was when I knew the group could do even better than it did, I recognized that his fairness and honesty enabled us to deliver consistently solid performance year in and year out.

Ultimately, his fairness was his most positive characteristic. I remember his demeanor during budget reviews, a time when many bosses would lose their cool and tear into people who had made money mistakes. These budget reviews tended to bring the worst out in bosses when things hadn't gone well; if they didn't particularly care for a direct report, this personal animosity would emerge during these reviews.

I never once saw the Good display this animosity, even when he didn't particularly like one of his direct reports. While he might be tough on someone because he was unprepared, he always was fair in his comments. His ability to set aside his personal feelings and deal with people based on what they did rather than who they were was rather remarkable, and it certainly endeared him to many of his people. Companies need Good managers as well as great ones; the former provides a solid foundation if not spectacular results.

TELLING TRAITS

Good managers live up to their name. The two things you notice about them right off the bat is that they're decent people who also are competent. Unfortunately, other types of bosses can be nice individuals and good at what they do, yet they're not Good. They may not be nice or competent consistently; they may not be genuinely nice but merely putting on an act; or they have other traits that are much more dominant than niceness and competence, putting them in another boss category.

So niceness and competence are simply the ante to get in the Good game. To identify this type of manager, you need to consider other factors or you're likely to misidentify someone as Good. One term that is useful as an identifier is "middle of the road."

Lucy, an executive with a financial services firm, exemplified this trait. In her five years with this firm, Lucy never fired a direct report. Nor did she ever single anyone out and actively campaign for this person to receive a significant promotion. Instead, she took pride in keeping her group together; she liked to maintain the status quo. In fact, people in her group joked about her performance reviews—they said that everyone in the group received a B+ and that she told everyone, "You've done very well, but you have the ability to do even better." She liked to keep her people happy, but she also expected them to meet deadlines and do B+ work. During a feedback session conducted by an outside coach, Lucy's group agreed that she was the most reasonable boss they ever worked for. They also agreed that their biggest disappointment was when Lucy refused to allow anyone in the group to participate on a cross-functional team that had been formed to explore a global business initiative. A number of her direct reports were excited about the opportunity, but Lucy felt that participating on the team was risky. She told an assistant that she feared that those who participated might be absorbed into a new division that would likely emerge from the initiative. She also expressed fear that her people would become too involved in the cross-functional team and that her group's performance would suffer.

To figure out if your boss is a Good type, think about the following questions:

- Does she believe in moderation in all things? Is she reluctant to be too harsh or too positive in her feedback?

- Are her meetings an exercise in precision and control? Does she move them forward quickly and professionally and make sure they don't devolve into endless debates or gripe sessions?

- Is she patient? Does she believe that "even this too will pass" when there is a major problem in the organization? Does she exhibit a saint's patience even when she's surrounded by sinners (i.e., evil executives or customers)?

- Does she favor the tried and true over the innovative but uncertain? Is she willing to entertain all types of suggestions and options but usually decides in favor of the safe course of action?

- Is she an advocate of logic and common sense? Does she call upon people to be reasonable and rational? Does she rarely allow her emotions to color her words or her actions?

- If she were a blind date, would someone describe her as a "nice gal," someone who is perfectly pleasant and intelligent but not someone who is particularly exciting? Is she one of the most predictable managers you've ever had?

INTERPERSONAL TACTICS: COPING WITH THE BOREDOM

Of all our managerial types, the Good probably is the easiest to deal with from a personal perspective. The Good's consistency creates behavioral expectations that are generally met, a far cry from Jeckyll and Hyde types. In fact, a number of people describe working for a Good manager as a "safe haven" from the games and pressures generated by other bosses.

Yet the Good manager is rarely a great manager, and this can create a different type of stress for people who report to him. If you're ambitious, if you like to be in the middle of the action, if you love testing new and innovative ideas—then you may bridle under the Good's firm grip. You may feel like you're stuck in a rut, that nothing exciting ever happens in your group. Boredom creates its own type of pressure, though boredom may be too strong a word to describe the environment in the Good's group. A more accurate description is a lack of challenge. Most people thrive when they are forced to learn new things and when they're pushed out of their comfort zones with assignments every so often. This doesn't happen regularly under the Good's auspices.

Therefore, the interpersonal tactics you employ to work effectively with the Good depend on your situation. If you're happy to work at a slow and steady pace for a consistent manager, then you need to focus on meeting the Good's rather modest expectations. If you find yourself bored to tears, you need to create your own challenges. Let's look at the former situation first.

First, recognize that the Good isn't a saint. He may be more tolerant than some other bosses, but he prizes reasonableness and control, and if you are unreasonable or out

THE GOOD

35

of control, he's not going to put up with it. So to meet the Good's expectations and develop a positive relationship with him, do the following:

- Meet modest objectives consistently. The Good depends on his people. He doesn't depend on them to come up with spectacular new concepts but to deliver decent results. If you don't let the Good down, he probably won't let you down either.

- Be transparent. The Good appreciates openness and honesty. Deliver both good and bad news concisely, clearly, and as soon as possible. Hidden agendas are a particular pet peeve of Good managers.

On the other hand, if you find yourself becoming antsy and requiring more challenge and learning than the Good offers, try these actions:

- Propose projects or experiences for yourself that are challenging. Recall that the Good was open to me taking acting classes, even though he would never have endorsed such a "radical" training method for the group. Good managers will be open to letting you pursue challenging activities as long as you make a good argument for them and it doesn't take away from your work performance.

- See if you can loan yourself out to other groups to do work that excites you. Again, the Good will probably be open to this idea as long as your work for his group doesn't suffer. If you possess skills or knowledge that are needed elsewhere in the company, your boss will recognize that he'll have another executive in his debt by lending you out. In turn, you have the opportunity to work on more challenging assignments. Take advantage of the Good's open-mindedness.

In terms of this second issue, the last thing you want to be is visibly angry or frustrated all the time. The Good wants his people to be happy or at least to seem happy. If you are demonstrably unhappy, this boss will be upset by it. He wants things to go smoothly, and he wants to believe that his people like working for him. If you can't find a way to moderate your anger or boredom, the Good will notice and do something about it. He may call in a coach to work with you, recommend a transfer, or even fire you.

PROFESSIONAL TACTICS: HOW TO WORK EFFECTIVELY FOR A GOOD BOSS

The Good boss provides clear, appropriate assignments for his people; they understand their roles and consider the time frames and scope of their assignments doable. The Good manager appreciates people who carry out their assignments effectively and demands little more than that from his direct reports.

Underneath this seemingly calm surface, however, problems roil. In big, steady, profitable companies, the Good often occupies a secure position and is able to protect his group. Because he usually delivers consistent results and few if any crises arise on his watch, management often leaves him and his people alone. Unfortunately, most big companies no longer are capable of steady, profitable growth. They are struggling, and because of their struggles, they are demanding more of their people—more risks to achieve greater rewards, more innovation to stay a step ahead of the competition, more team-oriented decision making to capitalize on diverse opinions and ideas, more speed and daring in executing strategies. The Good struggles in these environments, and if you're working for this type of manager, you may also struggle because the Good is better suited for a calmer, less challenging environment. Your group may not be able to perform up to the level management requires.

Even in more stable, less challenging environments, though, the Good can struggle with certain projects and assignments. The Good is not a particularly effective leader or manager when he's in unfamiliar territory. Unfamiliar subjects or stretch assignments push him out of his comfort zone, and he can become indecisive when decisiveness is required or rigid when flexibility is necessary.

If you're happy to be in a stable environment doing relatively unchallenging work, then you'll probably find that the Good manager is easy to work with. In other situations, however, you'll need to take certain steps to establish and maintain a productive relationship with this boss. Following are some suggestions.

WIDEN HIS NETWORK

This is the single best action you can take to help a Good boss. Good types aren't great networkers. They may be respected by the executives to whom they report, but they're often not very well known in the organization's nooks and crannies. In fact, they tend to make only the connections necessary to get their routine work done. They often feel uncomfortable with people outside of their function, with individuals who are working on projects they don't understand, and with "outsiders"—suppliers, customers, and others with whom they have little in common.

When you make the connections they lack, you open lines of communication as well as "supply lines" for needed resources. This is an especially useful endeavor in changing organizations where there's a need to connect with a more diverse group of people. Many times, the Good has problems knowing who has the expertise his group requires to carry out a stretch assignment or how to leverage that expertise. If you can develop a network, your contacts will be invaluable to the Good.

DECODE THE ORGANIZATION

Politics isn't the Good's strong suit. He is as far from Machiavellian as you can get. He doesn't understand how the MIS department works and is clueless when it comes to gaming the system in order to obtain resources above and beyond what is in the budget. Because the Good isn't particularly perceptive about areas outside of his area of expertise, he needs someone to decode people and processes. Be that individual and you'll not only help the Good function more effectively, but you'll prove yourself to be invaluable to this manager.

DEAL WITH THE BUSINESS AS IF IT WERE YOUR MONEY

This was actually a pet phrase of my Good boss. These Good managers prize fiscal responsibility, since it secures their place within organizations. They want their people to budget wisely and avoid the sort of overspending that gives groups negative reputations. Too often in organizations, people treat organizational money as "play money." They don't think twice about taking a customer out for a $500 dinner, while they would think long and hard about doing so if they were spending their own money. The Good doesn't mind his people spending money where appropriate and effective, but there has to be a solid return on investment. If you propose a project that costs x, you had better calculate how your return will be x plus and make a strong case that this return will happen. No one is perfect, and just about everyone makes some financial mistakes, but if you can demonstrate that you're generally responsible financially, you'll create the perception that you can be trusted with big (and costly) projects.

DO THE DIRTY WORK

Create a list of the tasks your boss dislikes revolving around confrontation and conflict, such as firing people; disciplining people; resolving conflict between team members; telling customers bad news; and handling an executive who is upset. No question, these aren't pleasant tasks, but someone has to do them for the group to function effectively. Volunteer for one of these dirty jobs and see how it goes. If you don't mind doing it and you do it well, volunteer for another one. Being a hatchet man for the good may not be the role you envision for yourself, but it can place you in the perfect position when you want the Good to recommend you for a promotion.

Donna, for instance, worked for a Good boss who headed a newly formed team in one of the world's largest companies. The company had recently restructured into teams that would facilitate faster decision making and more creative thinking, and the Good was a former functional manager who was put in charge of this team. Donna had come to the team with the Good, and she quickly realized that despite his intelligence and previous success as a functional manager, he was out of his depth as the team manager. He was unable to move the diverse group to a consensus; he would get bogged down in trying to be fair and let everyone be heard. He also was unable to control two members of the team who were overly negative—they tended to dismiss most of the group's ideas and convince everyone that a potential exciting project wasn't viable.

The Good recognized that he was having problems, and so he responded positively when Donna offered him a solution: appoint her to a position as his second-in-command, and give her responsibility for running the meetings. The Good knew that Donna was a tough, no-nonsense person who could be intimidating when she wanted to be, and so he accepted her offer. Within a month, Donna had maneuvered the two negative members off the team and had also established a meeting process that set forth clear rules (about time spent debating a decision, a method for achieving consensus, etc.). Donna enforced these rules, and very quickly the team became much more adept at getting things done.

BECOME A RISK MANAGER

As you should understand by now, the Good doesn't like to take risks. More than that, he likes to limit whatever risks he's forced to take by circumstance. Clearly, no one can eliminate risk entirely in organizations these days, and that shouldn't be your goal. You can, however, develop expertise at analyzing situations and communicating the risks involved. Help your boss determine

- What are the worst case scenarios?

- What are the options for action that might avoid worst cases?

- What can you do to avoid a given risky situation in the future?

You don't have to be a genius to be a risk manager. In fact, you don't even need to have any special ability to spot and manage risk. What you do need to do is develop a reputation for asking and trying to answer the previous questions. If you do this consistently, you'll be seen by the Good as a risk manager, and it will increase your value.

THE DON'TS: WHAT DOESN'T WORK WITH GOOD BOSSES

There are certain obvious ways to avoid getting on the Good boss's bad side, chief among them being a big risk-taker. Recognize that if you're working for a Good manager, you can't do anything your boss will perceive as reckless or highly speculative. You may have the best of intentions and be convinced your high-risk plan will pay off. You may even be right to take a risk—a situation may call for daring and innovation—but your manager won't agree. The Good views risk as capable of bringing down everything he's built, so it's wise to tailor your behavior accordingly.

When you present ideas and projects, make sure you address the risks involved in each of them. Don't assume the Good will understand that the risks are minimal or nonexistent. If you do make that assumption, you may find that a project is torpedoed because it seems to have uncertainties about it—at least that will be the Good's perception. By pointing out potential negatives and explaining how your approach will avoid them, you reassure the Good. Remember that the Good needs reassurance.

Less obviously, other don'ts include the following.

Don't Play Games

Other managers may countenance game-playing if these methods help achieve objectives. The Bully, for instance, would fully endorse game-playing direct reports if their manipulations and deceptions helped generate improved results. The Good, on the other hand, believes in straight talk and honest behavior. He hates being lied to. He doesn't like to be involved in office politics. He doesn't want his people to hide things from him. If you do any of these things and he finds out about them, his reaction will be to treat you like persona non grata. Unlike some other bosses, he probably won't become angry and chew you out for these behaviors, but he will give you the cold shoulder, which will impact the assignments you receive and your chances of being promoted or receiving a raise.

Don't Be Unpredictable or Inconsistent

Though the Bully and the Good have little in common, neither likes surprises. For the Bully, this is a command-and-control issue; for the Good, it's a matter of keeping things on an even keel. Good bosses want their people to be reliable. They want to feel secure in the knowledge that the individuals in their group will do what is expected of them. When people act out of character or their performance varies significantly, the Good becomes concerned. It's fair to say that the Good would prefer a consistent, mediocre level of performance than performances that swing wildly between great and poor.

Don't Pander

Good bosses want you to be yourself. They value authenticity and dislike phoniness. They don't like suck-ups and don't need you to tell them what a great decision they just made. If you're new to working for a Good manager, this "don't" may seem foreign to you. You may have worked for someone whose ego needed constant massaging or who expected you to conform to some role (i.e., an innovator, an aggressive go-getter, etc.). One of the strengths of Good bosses is that they relish employees who are comfortable in their skins. They accept people as they are rather than asking them to play a part. Of course, if someone is unpredictable, deceitful, or a gambler, they would prefer not to have him working for them.

CAN YOU MANAGE THIS BOSS TYPE? ASSESS YOUR OWN TOLERANCE

Here are two stories of individuals who worked for Good bosses but had very different reactions to them.

Rick, age 37, joined the corporate communications department of a midsized company after working for one of the world's top public relations agencies. At the PR agency, Rick worked on a number of high-profile accounts and was often dealing with one crisis or another. His boss at the PR agency was a highly demanding, highly volatile personality, and he frequently put enormous pressure on Rick to meet difficult deadlines and to handle members of the media who didn't want to be handled. This boss was an ex-newspaper editor who treated his direct reports like a stereotypical tough-as-nails newspaper man would, never saying a kind word no matter how well they performed. Though it was an exciting job with a great deal of visibility and a chance to advance his career, Rick was fed up after three years. He also was the father of two young children, and he found that when he returned home he barely had enough energy to play with them before they had to go to bed.

At the midsized company, Rick worked for Lisa, a Good manager. Right from the start, Rick relished having Lisa as his boss. Though the pace of work at this new company was much slower than that of the PR agency, the big difference was having a manager who was respectful and fair. Lisa didn't put on an act. As Rick said, "What you saw was what you got." Though Rick missed the drama of working in high-profile situations, he was willing to sacrifice the spotlight for a less stressful environment. Lisa demanded good work, but when she realized she could depend on Rick, she was flexible and complimentary in their interactions. If Rick needed to be home early to attend one of his kids' school events, Lisa was happy to accommodate him as long as there was nothing that needed to be done immediately. She also tried to help Rick and everyone in her group avoid late hours and impossible deadlines and overly difficult assignments; Lisa would intervene with management to prevent these things from happening. As a result, Rick arrived home from work at a reasonable hour and had the energy to be there for his children. As Rick said to his friends, "Lisa is the perfect boss for me at this stage in my career and my life."

Allison, on the other hand, found Jim, her Good boss, to be incredibly frustrating. They worked for a relatively young technology firm that was in a growth stage, and many opportunities existed for people to move up quickly—the company had a reputation for promoting people based on performance rather than seniority. Allison, who had done well at one of Silicon Valley's largest companies, had been frustrated by her slow career advancement. Confident to the point of cockiness, Allison saw the smaller but fast-growing tech company as a terrific career opportunity.

At first, everything seemed great. She liked Jim, thought him extremely knowledgeable about the organization and its products and dedicated to his group and creating a fun, innovative environment. Initially, Allison focused on becoming conversant with the organization and the way things were done. While she was on the learning curve, she was engaged and motivated. Being a quick study, however, Allison soon longed for the type of stretch assignments and blistering pace she enjoyed at her previous employer. She asked Jim to give her such assignments, and he obliged, but Allison's definition of stretch was different from Jim's. The challenges were modest, and she found herself growing bored. At her former company, Allison traveled around the world and liked the excitement of being thrown into situations that were literally and figuratively foreign. Jim, however, tended to keep his group away from such projects. He had carved out a niche for his team—they always came through with good but not exceptional work—and the CEO had said that Jim and his people were the "B players" that were the foundation of every good company.

Allison, though, hated being a B player, and within a year she had resigned and accepted an offer to return to her old job at her previous employer.

Are you more like Allison or Rick? To help you answer that question, make a check next to any of the following traits that apply to you:

Rick

- I relish predictability over excitement at work.
- I am much more effective when dealing with people who are logical than those who behave irrationally.
- I expect to be treated well if I demonstrate competency at a job.
- I'm at a stage in my career where I don't want a lot of stretch assignments, risky projects, and stress.
- I like being part of a team where everyone gets along and everyone from the most senior to the most junior member is treated respectfully.
- I do much better at a job when people ask me to do something rather than tell me.
- I prioritize job security over career advancement.

Allison

- If I'm given plum assignments, I don't care how hard I have to work or how much I have to travel.
- I can tolerate stress a lot easier than I can tolerate boredom.
- Learning and growth are my primary job objectives.
- I'm highly ambitious and want to work at a job that will help move my career forward.
- I'd prefer a boss with great clout and connections than one who is simply nice.
- I need to be challenged; if I'm allowed to do mediocre work, that's all I'll do.
- I measure my performance by promotions, salary increases, bonuses, and other perks; positive feedback really doesn't matter much.

To a certain extent, young people tend to be more like Allison, and more senior employees tend to be more like Rick. But this is a generalization, and I've observed just the opposite—the 58-year-old who is more gung-ho for challenge and risk than someone half his age, and the 27-year-old who wants nothing more than to be allowed to do his work in a calm, controlled environment. It's also possible that people move from an Allison mind-set to a Rick mind-set (or vice versa) because of some work-changing or life-changing event. A divorce makes them long for a stress-free work existence, or a mid-life crisis causes them to seek out jobs and tasks that push them to the limit.

The point is that you should know where you are at a given point in time and determine if a Good boss will be one with whom you can work productively and personally.

THE SECRET STRATEGY

Some people might think you don't need a secret strategy to manage the Good, since he's generally on an even keel. While it's true you may not have to do a lot to enjoy a pleasant relationship with him, be aware that your managing-up objectives should be higher. What you want is for the Good to view you as next in line for a promotion or to give you the assignments you need to further your career growth. You want to help him in the ways that count for him so he reciprocates in kind, and the Good will reciprocate; that's part of his nature.

Therefore, beyond the recommendations made earlier, your Secret Strategy should be:

Be indispensably dependable.

In other words, be the one person in your group who the Good can count on to do whatever it is that needs to be done. As noted earlier, figure out what the Good doesn't like to do (i.e., confront people) and fill that role. Be the direct report who always meets deadlines, follows instructions, and implements programs. The Good boss is reliable, and he in turn needs to rely on others. You don't have to be brilliant or innovative, but you do have to be there when the Good needs you. By positioning yourself in this way, you elevate yourself in the Good's eyes and have an inside track on getting the things you want from him.

THE KALEIDOSCOPE

Display Your Own Power

Selectively and Strategically

n dictionary definitions of a *kaleidoscope*, you'll often find references to complexity. This is an apt word to use when discussing Kaleidoscope managers. More so than the Bully or the Good, Kaleidoscopes are difficult to grasp, in large part because they shift from one persona to the next depending on the situation. Just when you think you have them figured out, they'll shift their style and you'll realize you really don't know them at all.

These shifts aren't random or a result of moodiness. Instead, they're calculated, designed to manipulate people and situations to their advantage. The K can meet with one direct report and be all sweetness and light, then meet with another direct report and be sour and dark. More subtly, the K boss can exhibit his sensitive side with a customer who needs to be listened to and display his decisive, commanding side with a customer who needs to be reassured.

Working for the Kaleidoscope boss is a challenge in that you feel like you're working for five different bosses, depending on the day of the week. You may find that he is generous and accommodating one day and indifferent the next. Even more confusing, you're never quite sure why he's acting the way he is. No doubt, he has a reason, but he's not likely to share it with you.

So what is the best way to deal with this complex boss? By recognizing that all the changes the K goes through are a result of his desire for power. Kaleidoscope managers often occupy the higher rungs of organizations because that's where the power is; or they may have jobs a few rungs lower but possess tremendous clout within the company, able to operate with an unusual degree of autonomy because of the power base they've created for themselves. They're like the Bully in that they're competitive and relish winning, but their style is completely different. They have control of their emotions; they intimidate and explode only if it suits their purposes. All their changes are focused on accumulating and solidifying their power rather than for ego gratification.

If you've ever had a Kaleidoscope for a boss, you probably didn't define him in your own mind from a power perspective. Instead, you may have privately called him Sibyl because of his multiple personalities. But it helps to understand that this boss isn't crazy, that there is a method to the seeming madness. He is after power, and when you can understand this motivation, you're in a better possible to deal with it.

First, let me paint a better picture of the Kaleidoscope by introducing you to the one I worked for.

THE KALEIDOSCOPE IN ACTION

My particular Kaleidoscope was a charismatic and compelling figure, and when he wanted to be, he could seem like a good friend. There were times when we would watch professional sports together, drink beer, and talk as if we were pals. And at first, I wanted to be his friend. Who doesn't want to form strong relationships with powerful people?

Yet as I discovered, the Kaleidoscope could turn off the charm as well as turn it on, depending on who you were and what he needed from you. When I transferred into his group, he was opposed to it; I was brought in only because his bosses thought I would add value. When we met, however, something clicked, and he became friendly and accommodating. What did I need? What were my goals? He asked good questions and backed up his words with deeds. With hindsight, I understood that our initial conversation revealed that my experience and expertise was something he could use. And the K was a user par excellence. He saw people as pawns to move around the board, and since he was a skilled chess player, he created the impression that they were knights rather than pawns.

The K had the knack of convincing people that they were his favorites. One executive in our group—we'll call him Steve—was sure he had been anointed as K's successor. K would spend hours each week with Steve, taking him out to lunch, sitting in his office talking business as well as about personal matters. They seemed inseparable, and K told Steve point blank how great he was doing and that he was his likely successor. Their close relationship lasted about five months, during which time Steve helped K with a number of sensitive projects. In fact, K's work on these projects was the major reason he received a promotion. After being promoted, not only was Steve passed over for K's job, but K treated Steve with a studied indifference—he no longer had any use for Steve's skills in his new position.

This description may make my Kaleidoscope seem heartless, but he wasn't a cruel or unfeeling man; he just believed that to gain power in a company, you had to use people. He expected those in power to use him. He saw nothing wrong with changing the way he related to people based on circumstance. With people in the lower ranks of the company, he tended to be a typical command-and-control leader, issuing orders and expecting them to be carried out. He was neither mean nor kind with them, since he could exercise his power in a neutral mode. With others—bosses, direct reports, customers—he was much more chameleon-like, adjusting his approach to fit in with what he was trying to accomplish.

The K reacted to people based on who they were and what they could do for or to him. He also was quick to assert his authority, especially if he thought it was being challenged in any way. If someone disrespected his authority—whether or not it was intentional—he had no problem putting him in his place. When I first joined the K's group, a big meeting was scheduled and I somehow misjudged the time it would take to get to the resort where the meeting was being held; I arrived 15 minutes late. When I entered the room, 20 people were already seated around a large table, and some of those people were the company's senior leaders. As soon as I sat down, the Kaleidoscope gave me a hard look, turned around to face the others, and said in a voice dripping with sarcasm, "Now we can start."

He wanted to assert his power, and he had a variety of assertive techniques, including a cutting sense of humor (which we'll address in more detail at the end of the chapter). If he had yelled at me, he would have come across to other executives as a petty tyrant. If he had asked why I was late, he might have seemed like an ineffectual school teacher. By using his sarcastic, dismissive humor, however, he positioned himself as someone in control. He demonstrated that he wasn't fazed by my late arrival yet he also communicated that he didn't like it and that there would be hell to pay if it happened again.

The Kaleidoscope also respected others who asserted their power and used it effectively. Once, I changed a procedure our group was using but didn't inform him of the change; he found out only when the new procedure was brought up for discussion during a meeting. Another time, I refused to present to a group that he had assembled because various delays resulted in my presentation being scheduled for late in the afternoon when a number of key members of the group had departed. I insisted it be rescheduled for the next day when the entire group would be there.

In both instances, the K wasn't pleased with my actions. I was disregarding his authority, and he didn't like such challenges to his power. For public consumption, he expressed his displeasure to me and others. Privately, however, he seemed impressed. He liked people who were assertive, who were confident enough in their own ideas that they took a stand. He respected displays of power, and so our working relationship improved significantly after these two incidents. Certainly, the Kaleidoscope expected people to respect his authority, but paradoxically, he also expected individuals to assert themselves regardless of that authority. Displaying the courage of your convictions earned you points with the K. Of course, your actions had to turn out right. If you flouted his authority and ended up wrong, you'd be in trouble.

Thinking back on my years working for the Kaleidoscope, what I remember most distinctly was his determination. No matter whether he was being charming, coldly authoritative, or argumentative, he took on his roles with great conviction.

No doubt, this came from his belief in his own power. He rarely displayed uncertainty or wavered on a position because he truly believed that might makes right. The K was more steadfast than many boss types. Because he radiated confidence and conviction, he had an aura about him. He could get away with shifting from one persona to the next without these changes being seen as political or crassly manipulative. People assumed that his shifts were designed to get what he and the group needed, and so they accepted them.

Of course, this determination and reliance on his power also proved to be the K's Achilles' heel. He was eventually promoted into a top job at the organization, but despite it being a high-level position, it was also one that restricted his power in different ways. The K was in a sensitive position, and this meant a number of "controls" were imposed on him. He needed approval before he took certain actions. His management team had to achieve consensus before it would implement certain plans. The board kept a close watch on what he was doing. Though the K had more positional power than he had ever enjoyed in his career, he also had less opportunity to use it freely. This made him unhappy and restless, and within a year of his promotion he resigned.

TELLING TRAITS

Identifying the Kaleidoscope is not always easy, since many organizational managers are ambitious and relish acquiring titles, responsibilities, and perks. Many managers also behave differently with direct reports than they do with their own bosses. Yet the K exhibits certain attitudes and behaviors that clearly identify him as a Kaleidoscope type.

Tim, the CEO of a midsized company, could be both a Bully and a Good manager at times, and he also had a bit of the Firecracker in him, but he was a Kaleidoscope because of the following:

- Every action he took and every word he spoke were designed to help him maintain and demonstrate his power.

Tim wasn't driven to leave a legacy. He didn't promote and make assignments based on a desire to help his people learn and grow. He wasn't motivated by a need to bring high-quality products and services to market. When Tim made a decision, it was all about power. For instance, he had to replace a division president, and he had three candidates for the job. One was relatively young but tremendously talented and committed. Another was a senior employee who had great experience and could be counted on to deliver good results. A third was not as talented or as experienced as the first two candidates, but he was the one Tim selected.

Why? Because this third candidate used to work at a company that Tim wanted to acquire, and Tim was sure that if he made this individual a division president, it would improve the odds that this acquisition would take place. Acquiring the company would give Tim and his organization more clout in the marketplace, and clout is another name for what Tim lived for.

Therefore, when trying to determine if your boss is a K, ask the following question:

- Is the primary motivation behind his action a desire to increase, solidify, or demonstrate his power?

Here are some additional questions that help you identify a Kaleidoscope:

- Does she shift personal styles with different people in the organization routinely in order to get what she wants?

- Does she possess self-confidence bordering on arrogance?

- Would you characterize this manager as self-controlled and controlling, as someone who always keeps her cool unless it is to her advantage to lose it?

- Is this individual one of the most intelligent and canny managers you've ever worked for? Does she always seem to know what to do to take advantage of a situation?

- Do you feel as if you don't really know this boss, even if you've worked for her for years?

This last question needs some explanation. Kaleidoscopes don't let their people know the real person behind their various masks. Their power depends on keeping others off balance. Is the real person the one who ingratiates himself to you in order to motivate you to do everything possible to close the deal? Or is the real person the one who is cold and indifferent when you're not needed for a project? The Kaleidoscope believes his power is diminished when people can identify him, so despite the trend toward transparency, the Kaleidoscope is resolutely opaque. Or rather, he may seem transparent if it suits his purposes, but the person he lets you see at one moment in time is often completely different from the one he lets you see in another situation.

INTERPERSONAL TACTICS: GOING WITH THE MANIPULATIVE FLOW

From a personal perspective, the most challenging aspect of working for a Kaleidoscope is the sense that you're being treated like a pawn in the game. As I noted, the K can make you feel like a knight rather than a pawn if he wants to, but over a period of time, you realize you're being manipulated—and no one likes being manipulated. It is unpleasant to feel like your boss is using you in some way and doesn't even trust you enough to explain how he's using you. Janice, a recent business school graduate at a recreational products company, worked for Dom and described him in this way:

When I first arrived at the company, Dom seemed like a good boss for someone like me who had little clout or experience. I noticed right from the start that other managers treated Dom with respect and even a little trepidation. He had an aura about him, and I figured that I would benefit by being in his group. And I suppose my career did benefit, since our group did well with Dom in charge and our accomplishments looked good on my resume. But I soon grew to dislike the feeling I got when Dom assigned me a task. Many times, he didn't disclose all the information to me. Instead, he gave me very specific instructions on what he wanted me to do and refused to give me a straight answer about why he wanted me to do it in a certain way. Once, he had me do a white paper on the poor quality of product parts we were receiving from one vendor; he instructed me to slant the white paper to indicate that the vendor's quality was even worse than it was. I later learned that he sent this paper to his boss and said that I had conducted an independent, objective study. It turns out that he wanted to get rid of this vendor and hire a friend's company, and my white paper gave him the ammunition to do this.

No doubt, this feeling of being manipulated is discomfiting, but if you're going to work for a Kaleidoscope, it's something you need to get used to. Here are some suggestions for coping with the feelings engendered by working for a Kaleidoscope boss:

ACCEPT THAT YOU'RE NEVER GOING TO KNOW THE REAL K

As frustrating as it may be to have a boss you can't figure out, it's even more frustrating to keep trying to know the unknowable. People who work in a Kaleidoscope's group spend much of their time together analyzing their boss, positing theories about his behavior and why he made a given decision. Similarly, they spend time alone parsing something the K said or did, going over it in their heads constantly in order to figure out "what he really meant." Recognize that the K will never let you see the real person behind the masks. Instead, accept that he will be a different person in different situations and work with each of the personas situationally.

DISPLAY YOUR OWN POWER SELECTIVELY AND STRATEGICALLY

This doesn't mean constantly challenging your boss and demanding things. When you have a powercentric boss, the last thing you want is to communicate that you don't respect or heed his authority; this is a sure formula for being fired.

On the other hand, you'll have opportunities working for the Kaleidoscope in which you can stand your ground and make your feelings known. This will earn his respect and make him treat you like a knight rather than a pawn. Following are some possible power-display opportunities.

When your stance or action doesn't have a serious impact on the K's authority. In other words, if you believe your group should be more aggressive in responding to a customer and your boss doesn't have a vested interest in a less aggressive approach, then this might be a good time to make your feelings known. Even if he's advocated a less aggressive approach, he may not be wedded to it. If you sense this isn't a big issue for him, state the case for what you believe.

When you can make a compelling argument that your recommendation will enhance his power. Perhaps you suggest that your group will win approval from the CEO if you take on a high-risk, high-reward project. Perhaps you argue for requesting a smaller budget than normal and working weekends in order to demonstrate the group's ability to work productively and profitably and receive a plum assignment that's coming up. The K will respond positively to arguments related to power and the person who makes these arguments.

When you tell him you don't understand and need things explained. Again, this is a tactic that should be used judiciously. If you're always saying you don't understand, your boss will think you're dense. The Kaleidoscope, though, likes to demonstrate his knowledge and why he's the boss. Power-focused people enjoy showing off what they know that others don't; again, knowledge is power. Ask him to explain a point he was making in a meeting. Request that he clarify the driving thesis in a white paper he authored. Communicate that you read the article he e-mailed you and you'd like him to provide you with more context about why he felt the article was important.

The Kaleidoscope can be among the most difficult of bosses to work for from a personal standpoint if you want him to be your friend, fail to grasp the role power plays in how he treats his people, and never let him show off his knowledge. If you master the tactics here, though, he can be relatively easy to deal with and won't cause you the sleepless nights that other managers might.

PROFESSIONAL TACTICS: HOW TO WORK EFFECTIVELY FOR A KALEIDOSCOPE BOSS

In one sense, most bosses are all about accumulating and using power. For this reason, bosses favor those who can help them acquire the symbols of power in organizations—better assignments, more resources, promotions, bonuses, and perks. Unlike the Kaleidoscope, however, other bosses have other interests. Some are driven by a vision of what the company or their individual group can achieve. Others are focused on productivity—on creating and sustaining a team that can function at a high level. The Kaleidoscope, though, is myopic about power, and it's wise never to forget this fact.

Unfortunately, it's easy to lose sight of this driver within the context of work life. Remember, the Kaleidoscope is difficult to know, and it may seem as if he wants to achieve a vision or build a great team. He's not going to tell you that what he's all about is building and using his power. You may think you're helping him achieve a significant work goal when, in reality, the K considers it a minor achievement compared to his power goals.

Therefore, working effectively with a Kaleidoscope means figuring out how your boss defines power and helping him within the context of this definition. Here are some tactics for doing so.

ENGAGE HIM IN A DISCUSSION OF WHAT HE HOPES TO ACHIEVE IN THE NEXT YEAR OR TWO

He may not be totally honest in his response—he may find it to his advantage to keep his aspirations to himself—but he may drop enough hints and innuendos to give you a sense of what is really important to him. Does he want a particular title in the company? Does he want to wield more decision-making authority? Is his main goal to defeat a rival in the company who is going after the same resources, people, and positions as he is? By identifying his most important goal, you are in a position to structure your work efforts in a way that helps him achieve it.

BE THE SOURCE OF INFORMATION HE REQUIRES

Knowledge is power. Given what his plans are for acquiring and consolidating power, you can keep him informed on issues related to that acquisition and consolidation. He may want to be informed of what is happening in a rival's department. He may relish information that gives him an edge on the company's budgeting plan or merger possibilities. He may need to know what talented people in other groups are eager to transfer into a new group.

Just providing your boss with lots of data isn't going to help you. In fact, the Kaleidoscope will probably perceive you to be nothing more than a researcher, and not a very good one, if all you do is feed him undifferentiated data. But if you can edit the data and tailor it to his purposes, you'll be seen as an asset who knows what is important in the organization.

Seed Ideas Rather Than Suggest Them Directly

Obviously, there are times when you want to make direct suggestions to the Kaleidoscope, but you should mix them with seeded ideas. That's because the Kaleidoscope doesn't want to feel that you, rather than he, is in control of the group's direction. You also don't want him to see you as overly ambitious and therefore a threat to his power. If, however, you master the art of subtle suggestion and the ideas you've seeded bear fruit, you'll gain stature.

By seeding, you create an unconscious dependence. He may not acknowledge that you're the source of the ideas that germinate for days or weeks in his mind and for which he claims credit, but the K is a smart person and realizes who is providing him with ideas he can use productively.

Prepare Him for the Roles He Likes to Play

Make a list of the key people he meets with: bosses, direct reports, customers, suppliers, consultants, and so on. Recognize that he is likely to take on a different persona or role depending on who he is meeting with and that you can educate him about what he might expect during the meeting. He likes to surprise people with his inside knowledge; it's a power game he plays. More than that, he wants to be able to play his role convincingly. If he's going to be a tough guy with a direct report who wants a raise, he needs to understand in advance how much the direct report is likely to ask for, what his rationale for the raise is, etc. If you have information about any of these issues, discuss them with the K. He'll be appreciative. More than that, he'll feel that you're savvy about the power games he likes to play.

THE DON'TS: WHAT DOESN'T WORK WITH KALEIDOSCOPE BOSSES

The don'ts are particularly important if you have a Kaleidoscope boss, since there are certain actions you never want to take if you work for this type of manager. To understand this last statement, consider Carlos, the entrepreneurial head of an ad agency. Carlos was the classic Kaleidoscope who created his ad agency from scratch by intimidating some and ingratiating himself with others. Any employee who had worked for Carlos over a period of time saw the different sides of him—they talked about "good Carlos" and "bad Carlos." In fact, Carlos had many permutations of both his good and bad personas, and he used them for a variety of purposes— to scare people into working harder, to get others to work harder in order to please him, to convince customers that he was brilliant, and to convince other customers that he would rather die than let them down.

All of these aspects of Carlos were designed to bring in new clients to his ad agency and increase the billings of established clients. Where his agency ranked in a magazine's annual survey of billings determined how Carlos saw himself. More relevantly, it measured the power he had in the industry. One day, two of his account supervisors came into his office and said they wanted a raise; they issued a veiled threat that if they didn't receive the raise they wanted, they would leave the agency and take a few key clients with them.

This was a huge mistake. They might as well have threatened to burn the agency to the ground. Carlos was apoplectic. He returned their threat with one of his own. If they did what they suggested, he would sue them for all they were worth; he would devote every last penny he had to bankrupting them through legal costs; he would use his considerable media clout to spread rumors about them that would tarnish their reputations forever. Whether Carlos meant any of this is beside the point. When he was in high dudgeon, he was a terrifying boss, and he managed to get both account supervisors to leave the agency immediately and without severance; needless to say, they took no clients with them.

If these two account supervisors had understood they were dealing with a Kaleidoscope, they would have rethought their strategy. The most obvious don't, therefore, is doing anything that threatens this boss's power base. Here are some other key don'ts.

DON'T TRY TO "PLAY" THIS BOSS

The Kaleidoscope is better at playing games than most. He's also skilled at spotting others who are trying to play games. The K wants you to do as he says, not do as he does. He may be able to get away with his power games and shifting personas, but don't try the same thing with him. If he suspects you're being disingenuous or are trying to manipulate him in any way, he'll call you on it. If you do it too much, he'll get rid of you. Being yourself, standing up for what you believe (as long as it doesn't threaten his power), and acting with authority and conviction are much better ways of dealing with this boss than through game-playing.

Don't Believe Everything He Tells You

He may mean it, he may not. Keep in mind that the Kaleidoscope will say what is expedient. His promises are made with a purpose. It's not that he'll lie to you intentionally but that he'll tell you what you need to hear so you do the task he wants done to the best of your ability. He can be very convincing, however, so you need to filter what he says with reality. He may promise you a promotion, but you have to ask yourself if he has the clout to deliver on that promise, if he's made the same promise to someone else, and if keeping that promise will help him maintain his power base.

Don't Forget That He Has Hidden Agendas

This last point is a bit more subtle than the others, but it can be a significant don't when you take his pronouncements at face value. He may make a big deal about how he endorses the team concept and wants more participatory decision making, but all this can simply be a sop thrown to management or a way to assuage team members who feel left out of the loop. If you forget this don't, you may speak out in an overly aggressive fashion during a meeting, and the Kaleidoscope will shoot you down in front of the group—he has no problem putting people in their place and cares not that you've been humiliated. The Kaleidoscope isn't a sadistic manager, but he does like to display his power on occasion, and if you misread his pronouncements, you may be on the receiving end of a cutting remark.

CAN YOU MANAGE THIS BOSS TYPE? ASSESS YOUR OWN TOLERANCE

Many people thrive working for the Kaleidoscope. Despite his obsession with power and the different masks he wears, he tends to be one of smartest, savviest managers people work for over the course of their careers. The art of using power and influence astutely can be learned under the K's tutelage. People who are ambitious and want to know how to handle a management position adroitly can pick up some important skills with the Kaleidoscope as a boss. Just as important, they can put up with the manipulation and control issues that can turn others off since they see them as tradeoffs—part of paying their dues.

The individuals who often struggle with the Kaleidoscope are those who seek a boss who is a mentor or father figure. They want to develop a genuine relationship with their managers. They want to feel like they understand this person and that this person cares about understanding and developing them. Above all else, they value transparency in a boss. The Kaleidoscope is more opaque than transparent, and he may help people in their careers and develop them, but that's not his top priority.

You may know from these two descriptions which category you fall under, but if you're still unsure, the following questions may help:

- Do you consider yourself highly ambitious? Do you want to learn lessons about office politics and other ways of advancing your career?

- Do you want a boss who can help you learn the ropes of how to be a decisive, effective leader?

- Are you able to deal with manipulative behaviors of a boss? Are you okay working for someone who isn't transparent or even particularly honest in all his dealings with his people?

- Do you view your jobs as means to an end? Are you more concerned with developing your knowledge and skills than in forming relationships?

- Is your primary goal to become an effective member of a team? Do you value the relationships you make in a job more than the perks you receive or your stature in the company?

- Are you looking for a boss who will take you under his wing and forge a relationship with you?

- Do you expect your manager to communicate with you, to listen as well as talk, to empathize and understand your problems?

- Do you believe you're most likely to succeed in your organization and your career through superior job performance, that a boss who can help you learn and grow is far more important than one who can teach you the shortcuts?

THE SECRET STRATEGY

The Kaleidoscope may seem like a serious person, but in fact he has a sense of humor and likes to work with people who appreciate his humor. While powerful people may come across as focused and intolerant of anything (including humor) that distracts from the task at hand, they often rely on humor as another way to demonstrate their power. Therefore, the unlikely but effective strategy with a K as a boss is:

Figure out what his sense of humor is and give him the opportunity to indulge it.

My Kaleidoscope, for instance, loved playing practical jokes. Some of them were clever and some were juvenile, but they all seemed to satisfy a need he had to trick others; it was another form of manipulation. If you'll recall my earlier story, my Kaleidoscope employed his cutting sense of humor to put people in their place. K liked people who could take and appreciate both his sarcastic remarks and his practical jokes. Going along with the latter was a requirement if you wanted to do well in his group.

Senses of humor vary, so make it your business to figure out the particular humor your boss enjoys. He may like telling jokes or hearing them. He may relish a sly, understated sense of humor. He may prefer the absurd—talking and hearing about all the irrational and strange events and policies that govern your business life.

Remember that the Kaleidoscope is a powerful but complex manager, and if you persist in trying to figure him out, you'll get nowhere with him. What you can figure out, however, is what makes him laugh. Being able to make him smile—or showing him that you appreciate what makes him smile—can go a long way toward helping you establish a relationship with this boss. It may seem like a small thing, but it's a small thing that matters to the Kaleidoscope.

CHAPTER

4

THE STAR

Enjoy the Ride

If you want fun and excitement at work, you've come to the right boss. The Star is one of those managers who make every day different from the one before it. He may insist that you and he fly to the other side of the world to observe the best practices of a high-tech Filipino company. He may issue a challenge to your team when you walk in the door that morning to come up with a fresh, money-saving approach before noon or "face the consequences." He may confront the CEO in the hallway and present a plan for restructuring the company and regaining competitive advantage.

Star bosses are dynamic and dramatic. They can also be difficult, but they're never boring. Working for them is like working for a world-famous celebrity—they know they're special and act the part. Stars also love to shake things up. They have no problem challenging the status quo, debating their own bosses, or trying something that has never been tried before. If you've had it with boring managers who cling to routines and adhere to all protocols, the Star manager will be a refreshing change. In fact, more than one person I know has said their best work experience ever was when they had Stars for bosses.

Of course, Stars rise and they fall, and if you're dealing with a falling Star, it can be an unpleasant experience. When things go south, Stars are quick to blame and insult. Their temperamental nature can make a job enervating as well as exciting. They don't have much of a governor on what they say or who they say it to, and if something goes wrong, they'll look for a convenient scapegoat. Stars vent when things don't go their way, and that may mean a tirade at a customer or at you. There are people who work for Star bosses who have been fired by them multiple times—it's their extreme response to stress. Even though they don't mean it—they hire people back minutes or hours later—it can be unnerving.

As temperamental as Stars can be, they actually are less volatile than The Bully and even the Kaleidoscope. Unlike these two managerial types, they are not particularly manipulative or bossy. What they are, though, is dramatic. As Stars, they like causing scenes. So if your Star boss does get angry with you, he may throw a flower pot at a wall rather than just chew you out. At the same time, the Star will clap you on the back, present you with a cigar, and tell everyone you're the most brilliant direct report he's ever had when you do something he approves of. Stars don't miss many opportunities to put on a show.

The Star I worked for was a true showman; he was also one of the most courageous, fascinating, and frustrating bosses I ever worked for.

THE STAR IN ACTION

At one point, the Star I worked for was considering an acquisition. Other people in the company told the Star that the acquisition was impossible, that too many obstacles stood in the way of it taking place. He ignored their warnings. In fact, he seemed to draw energy from all the objections they raised, wanting to show them they were wrong. The acquisition target was located in an unstable country, its owner and founder was a difficult man, and the company itself had run afoul of governmental regulators. No one doubted the potential synergies between our organization and this company, but everyone doubted that an acquisition would prove worthwhile.

With a zeal and a focus that can only be described as obsessive, the Star began to eliminate the obstacles. He made a number of visits to the company's headquarters at personal peril to himself. He courted the leaders of this company persistently, answering their questions and countering their arguments. He seemed to spend every waking moment gathering the support necessary to make the acquisition possible. During this time, working for him was like working for a man with a mission. He turned the acquisition into a crusade, and everyone in his group was swept up in his fervor. We drew inspiration from him and found him willing to do anything to help us. For most people who worked for him, it was the most exciting experience in our work lives to date. We felt as if we were doing something significant, something that would truly have an impact on the organization.

Of course, the flip side of this was working for a man who demanded more from his people than any other boss type. This translated into phone calls in the middle of the night and on weekends; expectations that you would miss your child's game or another school event to work on a business project; and a childlike impatience with delays or mistakes.

Stars also tend to be brilliantly analytical, which can be both helpful and hurtful for those who work for them. This particularly boss often demonstrated this analytical ability when presented with data. When he was presented with reports and especially with numbers, his mind would engage completely, and he was quick to spot the flaws in the analytical construct. On more than one occasion, I saw him challenge our CFO and tear apart a report and the financial conclusions it reached. Sometimes, this analysis helped produce a better outcome for the company. Sometimes, it was devastating to the people who compiled the report.

The Star tended to push his analysis too far. At times, he simply seemed to overanalyze for the fun of it. You'd present him with your findings and he would pick apart small inconsistencies or minor gaps, ignoring your larger conclusions that were valid and useful. As a result, he'd become enmeshed in the small stuff and lose sight of the big picture. This could be tremendously frustrating to his direct reports, who needed guidance but received nitpicking instead.

At times, the Star could be demonstrably kind, and in other instances, demonstrably harsh and unfeeling. Unlike the Kaleidoscope, little of this was calculated. The Star responded to people impulsively and often dramatically; at times he felt great empathy toward others and was not constrained about showing it, but at other times he could be indifferent or even cruel and didn't care if he was perceived negatively. In terms of the latter, one day the Star came to work and noticed that the ashtrays in the office were still full of butts—clearly, the person who cleaned the office had neglected to empty them. The Star was desperate and demanded that his assistant reprimand this individual. This assistant started trying to track down the cleaning person, and she discovered that she had died of a sudden heart attack during the night. When she informed the Star of this fact, he said, "And so who will clean my ashtrays now?" This assistant was shocked by his lack of empathy—it was disheartening to work for someone who showed so little compassion for others.

At the same time, the Star could show great compassion if the spirit moved him. In fact, this same assistant was a big fan of a famous singer, who was giving a concert in their city. This singer toured rarely, so it was a rare opportunity to see him. The assistant lamented that both she and her mother had heard this singer years ago, but they wouldn't be able to go this time because the show was sold out, and that even if it wasn't, the cost of tickets was prohibitively high. The Star found a way to acquire two premium seats for his assistant and her mother, paid for them himself, and hired a limousine to drive them to and from the concert.

Some people call this boss "bold"; others called him "foolhardy." Once, when he received a significant promotion, one of his first actions was to remove 70 percent of the 100 leaders who reported to him and replace them with much younger, less experienced executives. While many people may believe that a significant percentage of the staff they inherit isn't performing up to their standards, few would act on this belief. Fewer still would replace these terminated leaders with younger, less experienced ones. The Star, however, had tremendous confidence in his instincts. More than that, he was able to act on them. In this instance, his decision reinvigorated the entire organization—there was a lot of deadwood, and there was also a lack of young, ambitious leaders with tremendous commitment and energy.

When the Star's actions prove prescient, everyone hails him as a genius. When they prove to be wrongheaded, everyone says he's too impulsive and acts before he thinks. For these reasons, many people who work for a Star feel like they're working for an overly impulsive genius.

TELLING TRAITS

You don't have to look for subtle signs that your boss is a Star. Instead of the nuanced traits that help you identify some other boss types, the Star is clearly identified by a few telling behaviors and attitudes. Be careful, though, about confusing the Star with the Kaleidoscope or the Dreamer. All three are often confident and charismatic, yet the K is far more calculating than the other two, and the Dreamer is far less action-oriented. The Star also tends to make a show of everything he does, while the Kaleidoscope uses drama only in certain situations, and the Dreamer is more focused on articulating his vision or idea than in creating a drama around it.

With these points in mind, here are the key identifying traits of the Star.

HATES ANYTHING THAT DELAYS ACTION

Here's a simple test to determine if your boss is a Star. Place a check mark next to each of the following that he despises:

- Meetings
- Bureaucracy/red tape
- A series of presentations (to obtain approval prior to implementation)
- Slow software
- Discussions that circle endlessly around a point

- Indecisive managers
- Paperwork

If you made at least four check marks, that's a sign that you're working for a Star. The first item on the list—meetings—are especially galling to Stars. Observe their behavior during meetings. Do they fidget? Do they reprimand those who don't get right to the point? Are they intolerant of "speechifying"? Are they likely to nod off in other people's meetings? Do they often come up with excuses for not attending a meeting? Stars regularly exhibit these behaviors.

This type of boss is an implementer. She is more interested in executing strategies than tinkering with them. She is the classic woman of action, and when she is forced to sit and do nothing for long stretches, she may become as petulant or as bored as a restless child.

Is High-Energy

Other boss types may exhibit great energy in certain situations, but the Star always seems to be on. Naomi, for instance, was an attorney who ran a large corporation's legal department—a corporation, I should add, that was often involved in litigation with various parties. Naomi had seven attorneys working for her plus an outside firm, and as you might expect of a Star, she was a terrific litigator and negotiator. Though most attorneys are inherently conservative and cautious, Naomi relished taking aggressive stances and loved the verbal combat that sometimes ensued. The other attorneys found Naomi highly entertaining, and one of them said that she was "like a television show lawyer, always making speeches and making demands." Naomi also turned the company's battles with government regulators into epic struggles, using the media to make her case. She was a great interview, and she was especially good on television talk shows where guests debated the issues.

If Naomi had a downside in the minds of her people, it was that she lived for her work and expected her people to share her fervor. She worked six or seven days a week, and she expected her people to do the same. Naomi had tremendous stamina, and sometimes she forgot about taking breaks for lunch or dinner and had to be reminded by others of this fact. Her favorite phrase to her direct reports was, "You've got to keep up with me." Keeping up with her, however, was almost impossible, and the best the other attorneys could do was trail her without letting her get out of sight.

Like many Stars, Naomi was fully engaged with her job. It's not just putting in a lot of hours; it's an attitude that communicates the job deserves tremendous commitment and enthusiasm. While some managers may take a break during the work day and talk sports or politics or food, Naomi was always talking work. She talked fast and passionately about work subjects that she never seemed to tire of.

CHALLENGES THE STATUS QUO

It's difficult to know if Stars challenge the establishment because they truly believe it should be challenged or because they love to make waves. Whatever the reason, this trait is particularly useful as an identifier because not many managers in organizations are willing to confront senior leaders and tell them they're doing something wrong. The Star not only takes on these senior leaders but often does so directly and provocatively. While Stars aren't suicidal—they won't tell a CEO that his beloved strategy is stupid—they don't mince words. They can be politic while still communicating that they don't agree with an established policy or tradition.

Of course, they prefer it if they can inject some drama into the challenges. I've seen Stars deliver presentations that ripped long-established corporate cultures and philosophies, and they've done so when veteran executives who support these cultures and philosophies have been present. Somehow, their passion and eloquence help them escape censure or worse punishments because of these challenges. Many times, someone will say, "Oh, that's just Joe being Joe. He doesn't mean to be disrespectful." Stars earn a reputation for being willing to speak their mind, and many CEOs and other top executives value this quality and let them get away with things they wouldn't tolerate from other managerial types.

INTERPERSONAL TACTICS: LIVING WITH A STAR

Imagine working for Ralph Nader, Jesse Jackson, or some other charismatic leader of a cause-based organization. As loyal as their right-hand men and women might be, some of them must burn out. It is difficult if not impossible to match the energy of these leaders, to be as passionate and committed as they are, to deal with their impatience when things don't go their way. While they may be inspiring leaders, they also can be enervating to deal with.

If you have a Star for a boss, you know exactly what I'm talking about. More so than many other bosses, they provide both personal highs and lows. They create great excitement in the workplace, but they also demand a lot from their people. To cope with both the highs and lows, here are some effective tactics.

ENJOY THE RIDE

Working for a Star, your tendency may be to agonize about how you can't possibly put in the hours or provide the level of commitment your boss expects. You may worry you're going to let your boss down. You may feel bad when he suddenly turns on you because he is so impatient with the slow pace of a project.

This is the wrong attitude for anyone who has a Star as a boss. If you focus only on the down side of working for this manager, you're not going to be happy. Invariably, you will let this boss down in some way—you can't possibly keep up with him. No one can. All you can do is do your best and accept that there will be times when your best won't be enough for him. Of course, no one's best will be sufficient, so recognize you're in the same boat as everyone else.

A far better attitude is being aware that working for the Star is a blast and that you should relish every moment of drama that comes with the job. By "enjoy the ride," I mean you should have fun riding on the Star's coattails. Laugh at his outrageous stances. Take pride in being part of his crusades. Sit back and be entertained by his performance. Few bosses will provide you with ringside seats to a great show, so let yourself enjoy it by not worrying all the time about your own performance.

TRY TO STEER RATHER THAN CONTROL

This means that there will be times when you can steer your boss in the right direction with suggestions. Sometimes, even steering is impossible, and you're just going to have to let this manager do his thing. Still, it helps to realize that while this manager is uncontrollable, you can exert influence.

One of the great frustrations of working for a Star is that his own internal voice overrides the voices of others. He has such a strong will that he will bull forward even when common sense and all the voices around him tell him to stop. If you try and control this boss, you're going to find yourself in a no-win situation. Making good arguments, showing him the facts and figures that prove your case, gathering others who agree with your point of view—these tactics may work with other bosses, but they won't work with the Star.

Jessica had recently received her MBA, and she joined a large packaged goods company. Her first boss was Jack, a Star of the first order. Jack wasn't that much older than Jessica, but it was clear to her that he was on the fast track, and she was excited about the possibilities for her career because she was part of Jack's team. Dynamic, decisive, and tremendously insightful about the business, Jack was respected and admired by managers many years his senior.

Yet after a year of working for Jack, Jessica was fed up. On at least three occasions, Jack had pushed projects that Jessica knew had no chance of success. On the third of these projects, she mustered her courage and told Jack it wouldn't work. He brushed her objections aside, and it irritated her how brusque he was and how wrong he turned out to be. She kept telling her colleagues and friends, "If only Jack would listen to what I have to say, our group would deliver far better results." The words *if only* often prefaced her remarks about her boss, and they reflected her increasing frustration.

Finally, Jessica found a way to diminish this frustration. She discovered that if she happened to choose the right moment to speak to Jack about one of the projects he fiercely believed in, he might adjust his approach based on her input. Generally, the earlier in the process she spoke to him, the better able she was to steer him in the right direction. If too much time passed and Jack had worked himself into a lather over it, nothing she said would make a difference. He also listened better in nonwork settings—lunch was a great time to get through to him. By adjusting her approach and setting her expectations a bit lower (in terms of how much influence she could wield over him), Jessica found it much more satisfying to work in Jack's group, and the group's results also improved because of the adjustments Jessica made.

BE PRECISE

Patience is not this manager's virtue. The Star wants his information quick and neat. Long or unclear explanations will irritate him to no end. Certainly there are times when you can engage in longer conversations with the Star—in fact, Stars sometimes are needy for company and conversation. But you have to be alert when Stars are stressed and flying high and fast. In these instances, they have little tolerance for you going off on tangents or providing unnecessary context. Get to the point, and they'll appreciate your brevity. More importantly, you'll find them easier to deal with when they're in high-stress mode.

PROFESSIONAL TACTICS: HOW TO WORK EFFECTIVELY FOR A STAR BOSS

As the name implies, this boss likes to shine, so your job in part is to help him maintain his star status or to make him an even brighter star. This doesn't mean you do his job for him—he'd hate that—or even that you provide him with great ideas he can claim as his own. Instead, working for a Star is much more of a support role than for some of the other boss types. You're a sidekick, a makeup person, a flack, a trusted assistant. This type of boss doesn't need or want a direct report who functions as an equal or almost an equal. His ego is big enough and his belief in himself is strong enough that his most valued subordinates are supporters rather than contributors.

I'm not minimizing this support role. To a certain extent, support is important to working with all boss types—it's just more important for this particular type. With this role in mind, here are some tactics that will help you provide the support your boss needs and that will help you work well together.

BE A PATIENT LISTENER

Stars need an audience. Listen attentively and ask good questions. This will help you know where your boss needs assistance, and it will help her vent her negative feelings as well as release some of her pent-up energy. It will help you gain an understanding of her and learn what ticks her off and what makes her tick. She may never come to trust you in the way a Good boss would, for instance, but she'll feel more at ease with you, which will facilitate your working relationship.

ASK FOR HELP

Unlike some other managers, this one loves it when his people ask him for assistance or tell him they're struggling with an assignment and need his guidance. He likes being put in the position of authority and knowledge. There are instances when he won't be responsive to requests for assistance—he's too wrapped up in his own issues—so you need to be aware of what's going on in your manager's business life. But when you truly don't know something and you could benefit from his expertise and experience, take advantage of this aspect of the Star's personality. He'll be appreciative that you asked, and you'll probably gain valuable advice.

PROVIDE POST-GAME ANALYSIS

Stars may not want your analysis prior to making a decision or launching an initiative, but they may want it afterward, especially if their project didn't work out as planned. Stars don't want to hear what was wrong with their ideas but where their projects went wrong. Who prevented the launch of a new policy from being successful? Was it a lack of sufficient funding that resulted in a less-than-optimal software purchase? Did they fail to make the sale because a customer wanted a larger vendor? As long as your analysis focuses on what others did wrong rather than what the Star may have messed up, your boss will find your input useful.

RESPOND QUICKLY

Stars place a priority on speed. Like little kids, they hate to wait. If they request a report by Friday, have it on their desk by Thursday. If they ask a question, don't hem and haw or say, "I'll have to get back to you on that." Learning to think on your feet is a valuable skill from the Star boss's perspective. Rightly or wrongly, he believes that people who respond quickly to his requests are his most effective people. They're the ones who receive the best assignments and are most likely to be promoted.

The first and most crucial don't is:

DON'T BE DISLOYAL

If you want to see a Star boss fly into a rage and treat you like a leper forever afterward, betray his trust. Art worked for Marcel, the CEO of a small but very profitable company. He had worked for Marcel for five years and had benefited greatly by serving essentially as Marcel's right-hand man. Marcel, a Star, was also the company's founder, and it had flourished largely because of his charismatic leadership. Art liked working for Marcel and had accepted Marcel's ego and grandstanding. Even though he wished he were given more credit for his contributions, Art enjoyed the dramatic environment Marcel created and believed he was fairly compensated for his efforts.

At a trade convention Marcel and Art attended along with other company employees, Art ran into the CEO of a competitor whom he had gone to business school with. Art and this competitor had been good friends but had lost touch, so Art was delighted to see his old friend at the trade show. They went out to dinner that night and had breakfast the next morning. Art had to miss a breakfast with Marcel and some customers, and he had requested permission to do so from Marcel beforehand, telling him only that he had run into an old friend. Marcel later found out that the old friend was a competitor, and he was furious. From that day onward, Marcel never treated Art the same way. Though he didn't fire him, he no longer confided in him or brought him to key meetings or on important business trips. To Marcel, breakfast with a competitor was a betrayal.

Stars are more sensitive in this area than other boss types. They define disloyalty in broad terms. Turning down a trip or an assignment, attending a family function rather than the company holiday party, making a slightly negative remark that seems to contradict what the boss said—all of this can be construed as disloyalty, even if it was not meant to be disloyal.

DON'T BE A WET BLANKET OR A NAYSAYER

Some bosses like their people to raise worst case scenarios, to serve as fail-safe systems in the event they've missed something in their planning. Star managers, on the other hand, possess a certain hubris. They believe in their ideas absolutely. Point out the flaws in their reasoning or warn them about negative outcomes consistently and you'll alienate Stars.

Think about how many times you start a conversation with this boss by saying, "Have you considered what might happen if . . ." or "If I were you, I'd think twice about . . ." or "The risks outweigh the rewards." You may not be a negative thinker—you may in fact be raising appropriate red or yellow flags—but you'll come off as a doom-and-gloom person, and the Star won't want you around. To the Star, you're not just questioning his idea—you're questioning who he is, and his hubris won't tolerate it.

If you really feel he's making a serious mistake, find an indirect, nonthreatening way to warn him. E-mail him an article on the subject and suggest he might like to read it. Preface your remarks by saying something disarming, like, "I know this is probably nothing, but . . ." Or be positive about aspects of his plan but point out what might detract from its one questionable area. In this way, you don't seem like

THE STAR

a negative person and you are more likely to penetrate his hubris.

Don't Talk Back

Some bosses you can argue with. Some like to engage in debates and respect your right to voice your opinion, even if it's at odds with theirs. Stars may allow you one mild objection or smart-aleck retort, but they won't let you get away with much. If they believe you're being disobedient or disagreeable, they will be turned off. They won't have the patience to deal with you.

Stars may say they want feedback and honest opinions, but what they really want is obedience. Don't fool yourself into believing your Star boss values your opinion more than others and that you can get away with engaging him in endless debates while others can't. If you protest or voice your opinion and it has no impact, let it go. You're not going to break through no matter how hard you argue or how brilliantly you articulate your point of view.

CAN YOU MANAGE THIS BOSS TYPE? ASSESS YOUR OWN TOLERANCE

Let me emphasize that I truly enjoyed most aspects of working for my particular Star manager. I watched him move up in the organization in a way that wasn't dependent on who he knew or political game-playing as much as his supreme confidence and charisma. At his best, the Star was the type of leader I and others willingly followed into battle. He had an egalitarian aspect that I haven't really communicated, but it earned him a lot of respect. He was just as likely to chew out a

CEO as a subordinate, and just as likely to praise either one. Many times, you work for a manager who you like but don't have a great deal of faith in. That wasn't the case with the Star. His swashbuckling style, his willingness to say and do anything that had to be said and done, and his business intelligence all made him a pleasure to work for.

Does the above paragraph sound like something you'd say or wish you could say about your manager? If so, then this may be an ideal boss for you. Here are some additional questions that will help you assess your tolerance for a Star.

ARE YOU A GOOD SOLDIER?

In other words, can you take orders well and without question? Some people can't, especially younger people. They want to know why before they'll take on a task. They want the freedom to challenge the why if it doesn't meet their requirements. On the other hand, if you're a good soldier and take satisfaction from the triumphs of your team, then the Star might be a good manager for you. An analogy is the free agent professional athlete who has a chance to sign with two teams: one will give him a good shot at winning the championship, and the other will give him complete freedom to play the game the way he wants and be in the spotlight. The latter would not do well working for a Star boss—he wants to be the star himself. Other people, though, derive great satisfaction from being in the background and helping their boss and group achieve tremendous results.

DO YOU LIKE DRAMA IN YOUR WORKPLACE?

Not everyone does. Some people prefer environments where calm and consistency prevail. They hate battles, crises, and unexpected events. They don't want to plunge into a project up to their neck and be told it's sink or swim.

Other people find this type of environment energizing. They often refer to their workplace as an "insane asylum" or as a "circus," but they do so with a certain amount of pride. Pam, for instance, worked for a Star manager, Ginny, who she was convinced had ADD. Ginny was constantly in motion, pacing during meetings, running to catch planes. When she was seated for a one-on-one conversation, she would invariably spring from her chair when she had a point she wanted to emphasize. Ginny would involve her staff in what she called "missions." Sometimes, they'd pull all-nighters trying to come up with viable ways to make an initiative work. Sometimes, they'd fly on a moment's notice halfway around the world. Pam said there were also frequent confrontations. Once, she, Ginny, and another member of their team met with one of their largest customers and issued him an ultimatum: either he increased the amount of services he purchased so they met Ginny's requirements, or they would resign the account. As Pam said, Ginny created a lot of tension regularly, but she also made sure her people were constantly challenged and involved, which Pam loved.

DO YOU ASPIRE TO BE A STAR YOURSELF?

It doesn't always hold true that the people who do best working for a given boss type are just like that boss themselves. In fact, if you're a Bully, you probably will fail miserably working for a Bully boss because you'll constantly be marking your territory and fighting. But stars-in-training are well suited for groups run by Stars. They like the dramatic atmosphere this boss creates. They enjoy watching a Star in action, observing what this type of boss can get away with that other managers can't. They also tend to "get" their bosses in ways that other people don't; they instinctively recognize that Star bosses need their support rather than their ideas or their challenges.

Therefore, think about how you might run a group. Would you be the type of boss who reflexively challenges people, processes, and procedures? Would you create a lot of drama as you introduced new ideas or implemented new strategies? Would you work at a fever pitch and with unshakable confidence as you moved your agenda forward? If so, then you probably will enjoy your time working for a Star and perform well under his tutelage.

THE SECRET STRATEGY

People often assume that Star managers need to be flattered. They figure their egos are sufficiently large that they require constant care and feeding. In fact, most Star bosses hate sycophants. They are sufficiently perceptive that they know brown-nosers when they see them. While they don't want their people to disagree with them or point out their weaknesses, they also prize people who are authentic. They value and need other people. They love an audience, especially an audience that genuinely appreciates their performance.

Therefore, the secret strategy here is:

Be a supportive friend to your boss.

In my experience and from observing other Star-subordinate relationships, I've found that these managers don't choose the most quiescent or complimentary direct reports as their right hands, but those to whom they can relate. They work best with the individuals who get them, who like their sense of humor, who are impressed by their daring, who can lend them a sympathetic ear (which is why I emphasized listening as a key professional tactic).

You're not going to be able to fake this strategy. To be a supportive friend to the Star, you need to like his style and substance. If you do, then approach the Star as a friend, albeit as one who gives more than you take. Be there when he needs to vent. Go out to lunch with him and listen to his stories. Ask him the sorts of questions that allow him to think out loud, to analyze a situation.

In this way, you can form a bond with a Star boss that will not only help you work productively in the present but possibly create a mentor for life. Remember, loyalty is a major value for Star bosses, and if you give it, you'll receive it in return.

THE SCIENTIST

5

Enjoy the Intellectual
Challenges

If you think of business as a giant laboratory, then you'll recognize the Scientist as the person in charge of the experiments. Rather than experiment with test tubes and chemicals, this manager relies on management theories and concepts. In my experience working for the Scientist, I noticed that he seemed most happy when he was putting a favored leadership or management theory into practice or testing a new theory of his own devising. When I worked for him, I felt I was working for someone who had a brilliant if somewhat academic grasp of the way business functioned.

As the name implies, the Scientist has a head for business theory. In many cases, this manager has gone through a top MBA program, put in time at a major consulting firm, and perhaps even spent some time in academia. He loves business books and the latest management fads, and especially likes talking with his people about them. This doesn't make him a bad manager and in fact can make him a very good one if he's using the right business concept for the right situation.

At times, though, he is too much in love with the theory of business and not in love enough with its practice.

The Scientist talks a good game. He has a keen mind and a tremendous grasp of theory and practice. He is utterly convincing when he speaks about a subject he knows well and believes in. Even if he's not eloquent, his passion and knowledge come through and do a good job of getting people to climb on board. He may not be charismatic like the Star or a master wielder of power like the Kaleidoscope, but his intellect and ideas confer on him a certain stature within the organization.

I should add that the Scientist enjoys the gestalt of work. Unlike some other managers, he doesn't come to work angry, cynical, or scheming. Instead, he usually likes his bosses and his direct reports, the meetings, the business trips, the presentations. Again, our analogy is apt: just as the scientist is at home in the lab, this business Scientist is at home in the office. More so than most boss types, the Scientist is a relaxed manager, comfortable in his own skin. A collegiality exists between the Scientist and his people; he fosters a sense of shared purpose and an esprit de corps.

If all this sounds ideal, let me note that sometimes the Scientist's experiments blow up, and working for this managerial type in these situations can be difficult, to say the least. I should also add that some Scientists can turn into Mad Scientists, especially when their experiments go awry or their bosses disagree with their techniques.

The best way I can communicate both the positive and negative qualities of this boss type, however, is by giving you a closer look at the Scientist I worked for.

THE SCIENTIST IN ACTION

My Scientist was a civilized, social man who had done very well in his career. When I worked for him, he had great, global responsibility in a large company and was being groomed for even grander things. When he was brought in, management saw him as a forward-thinking leader, one who had a clear theory of the case and could articulate it convincingly.

When I write that this man was civilized, I mean that he enjoyed intelligent discussions with his people. Some leaders make a great show of listening but don't really hear anything you say. The Scientist listened and absorbed. He actually liked feedback, and even if it wasn't complimentary, he valued it. On Friday afternoons after our regularly scheduled management lunch, I would sometimes join him for a glass of wine in his office before leaving for the day. He always had excellent French wine as well as excellent conversation to go along with it.

Most of the time, our talks focused on business issues, and we would discuss things at a high, conceptual level. Once, the Scientist shared with me his belief in the viability of a well-designed team. He was convinced that if the team were constructed properly—that if best practices were followed—then it would always function well even if some of the key people departed. His belief in "right design" was almost religious, an odd thing for a man of science. Yet it was indicative of how much faith he placed in overarching business principles. He was like other business Scientists I've known who are fond of referring to a higher power in justifying their decisions, be it a pioneering business leader, an academic, or a famous case history. Instead of responding instinctively to situations or through the use of power, they would gravitate toward a larger principle to guide their actions.

This particular Scientist loved being placed in situations that allowed him to test his beliefs. At one point in his career, he did particularly well as head of a unit and received a promotion to a significantly more challenging job. Though the Scientist liked the fact that he was promoted, he liked even more the opportunity to test his ideas in a new setting. He worked in order to experiment, and a new, more challenging position provided him with the chance to do so.

As a Scientist, this boss believed in conveying information objectively. He didn't say things to be mean or manipulative, but he believed in stating the facts as they were. His complete lack of artifice when providing feedback softened whatever negative remarks he might make. Once, he told me, "You're not smart enough to run this project." Coming out of other managers' mouths—such as the Bully's, for instance—such a comment would have been hurtful. The Scientist, however, kept emotion out of his voice, and the matter-of-factness of his delivery helped cushion the blow. If anyone was skilled at delivering bad news, it was the Scientist. On more than one occasion, he told people that they wouldn't be getting a bonus or a raise, and the people accepted it because he would explain why without being pejorative or emotional. His directness was disarming. People talk about the importance of transparency for leaders today, and the Scientist was naturally transparent.

One of the great things about working for a Scientist is that he lacked the pretense of many other managers. He treated just about everyone as equals. He was perfectly happy to take his management team on wonderful trips and relate to each and every one of them as friends as well as colleagues.

Part of his business theory was the importance of collegiality to teamwork, so he didn't pull rank and instead treated each of his direct reports as individuals rather than as cogs in a machine. He also understood the importance of fun to morale, and he made it fun to work in his group.

Though I noted that my boss didn't mince words when he needed to state a hard truth, he also was supportive to a point. I'll explore where this point ended later in the chapter, but here let me stress that you could count on this Scientist to provide you not only with some support in terms of advice and resources but emotional support as well. Once, I made a presentation to 50 other corporate executives, and it went poorly, in large part because I had delegated significant responsibility to one of my own direct reports, and he wasn't ready to handle it. After the meeting, the Scientist invited me into his office to discuss what had taken place. In a similar situation, the Bully would have chewed me out, the Kaleidoscope would have given me the cold shoulder, and the Star would have delivered a lecture. The Scientist, however, poured me a glass of wine and said, "That wasn't so great, was it?" We both laughed and were able to talk about the meeting in a way that I learned from my mistake and didn't feel bad about it. The Scientist helped me recognize that not all experiments work, and all you can do in these instances is shrug off the failure after a drink and some laughter.

Because not all experiments work, however, the Scientist was a frustrating boss to work for at times. He was adamant about sticking with the experiment past the point most reasonable people would have deemed it a failure and moved on. This created tension; from the Scientist's perspective, you were either with him or against him. There were times I found myself supporting the Scientist's programs and policies out of loyalty even though common sense told me they weren't working. There were also times I had to try to mediate for people who had been negatively impacted by the Scientist's failing programs, and though he was always willing to listen, he was rarely willing to give up his belief in these programs.

TELLING TRAITS

The Scientist could be confused with the Good or with the Kaleidoscope in some instances, since all three are the types of managers that people generally like working for because of their people skills. Yet the Scientist is a distinct boss for a number of reasons, not the least of which is his fervent belief in some theory or system as justification for his actions. As soon as you see a manager who espouses supply chain theory at every opportunity or talks about matrix management as if it were a religion, the odds are good that he's a Scientist.

To help you in your identification process, here are some additional traits that a Scientist possesses.

A BIT OF A PEDANT

In other words, Scientists love to expound on their management theories. Mark, for instance, was a middle manager who worked for a company that was involved in a lot of controversies, and he was a proponent of "bend over backward" crisis management. His belief was that companies do themselves no favors by stonewalling the media, and that they serve both themselves and their stakeholders better by being completely transparent and responsive to the media. Mark, who was in the marketing division, put his crisis management belief into practice whenever his group found itself in emergency situations. More than that, though, was that he would talk about this belief at the drop of a hat. He wrote a white paper on the subject that he posted on the company's Web site; he requested a meeting with a senior vice president to present his views; and he lectured his own people about the validity of his approach. Mark was smart about crisis management and even eloquent at times in defense of his beliefs, but he could go on too long and a little stridently about this subject.

Most Scientists aren't boorish in arguing their theories, but they can come across as slightly obsessed teachers in their manner. They are so fervent that at times they fail to place a reasonable limit on how long and how often they talk about these issues.

OPERATES WITH A THEORY OF THE CASE

Scientists have a reason for making decisions or taking significant action. These are not seat-of-the-pants people but managers who frame their choices in larger theories or concepts. It's likely your boss is a Scientist if he refers to books, business theoreticians, or business models when explaining why they're doing what they're doing. They don't refer to these models and authorities defensively or to show off their knowledge but because they believe in them. They enjoy talking about them and demonstrating how theories and concepts apply to real business situations.

FEEDBACK-FRIENDLY

Scientists are big believers in feedback—both in giving and receiving it. Like any good science person, they value dialogue around topics of value to their work. Therefore, they usually make the time to talk to their people about how they might be more effective and listen to feedback from them that might improve the group's efficacy. They may not always agree with what you have to say or suggest, especially if it doesn't fit with their theory of the case. But they will listen.

Also, this feedback is delivered in an emotionally neutral tone. As I noted earlier, they like to communicate directly and objectively. Unlike other managers, the Scientist is non-judgmental, preferring to deliver the facts rather than to assign blame. While the facts can be harsh—they won't mince words if the numbers are down or if there's a clear pattern of mistakes in your work—their feedback will stick to the realities of a situation rather than all the politics and personalities involved.

SOMEWHAT DISORGANIZED AND DISTRACTED

Most managers are relatively buttoned up—they are good at running meetings, meeting deadlines, and sticking to schedules. Scientists, however, are different. They may allow meetings to drag on or go off on tangents. They may also abruptly cancel meetings because there is something else they decide is more important—and it may not be more important to the group but to whatever they are obsessing about at the time.

Scientists are also notorious for getting a glazed look sometimes during conversations. As much as they value their people and their contributions, they are focused on concepts more than anything else. It's almost as if they have so many thoughts buzzing in their heads that they can't always be 100 percent attentive to you or even to their own bosses.

I don't want to make Scientists sound like absentminded professors, since they wouldn't last long in top positions if they never seemed to be paying attention. But every so often, they exhibit qualities that are more characteristic of academics than of business professionals. In fact, these qualities are tolerated by management. This tolerance is usually expressed when someone says, "Yes, John can seem like he's not paying attention at times, but he so incredibly smart he's probably thinking up something that will help the business."

INTERPERSONAL TACTICS: FORMULAS FOR GOOD SCIENTIST RELATIONSHIPS

Scientist managers are relatively easy to get along with, especially if you subscribe to their theories. Because Scientists are even-keeled and not overly demanding—and because they are good communicators and treat their people well—they are the type of boss most employees are eager to work for.

The reality of working for them, however, isn't always as ideal as it may appear. As much as I enjoyed being part of the Scientist's team, there were instances when his approach to work was frustrating. Changing situations could have a profound effect on this manager's style, more so than many other managerial types. Generally easy to deal with during good times, the Scientist can become distant, moody, and difficult during bad times. Scientists in general have a lot of success in organizations—they're smart, aggressive people who are valued by management. So when a project they're heading fails or runs into problems, they're not used to it and often react badly. I found this to be the case with the Scientist I worked for. As long as things were going his way, he was accommodating with his time, ran his group in a relaxed manner, and shared the glory when objectives were achieved. But when we hit a snag, he became a much more tense and introverted person. In a few instances, he became another managerial type entirely, squeezing his people for profits like the worst sort of Bully. It was almost as if bad times unhinged him temporarily; he didn't know what type of manager to be when things went wrong. This was particularly disturbing to the people in his group who were close to him—we felt like he wasn't acting normally, and it was upsetting.

With that as preamble, here are some tactics you can use to make working for a Scientist a personally rewarding experience.

ENJOY THE INTELLECTUAL CHALLENGES

Not every manager is as smart and as sophisticated in terms of business principles as the Scientist. Too often, we find ourselves working for someone who isn't as smart as we are or who is smart but dull in his approach to business. The Scientist provides his people with a theoretical framework in which to work, giving them assignments that require thought and discussion.

Joan was a Scientist of the first order, the CEO of a rapidly growing but still relatively small database management company. Joan was brilliant, but she did not have the usual business pedigree. In fact, she was an English major as an undergraduate at a prestigious East Coast school and had gone on to get her Ph.D. in philosophy. She had started out as a professor but had quickly tired of academia and disinterested students and become fascinated with the world of business, working for a direct marketing company and then for a consulting firm. Joan had written a number of articles about management and business strategy as well as one book.

While most of Joan's people enjoyed her style and her personal warmth, some found her rigid to the point of

THE SCIENTIST

self-destructiveness when it came to certain business situations. For instance, Joan advocated being completely open and honest with customers; she insisted that her people tell customers whenever mistakes were made and provide them with a plan to avoid such mistakes in the future. Obviously, one of her business tenets was transparency. Once, her company made a mistake in the design of a database management system that had no impact on the customer; they never would have known a mistake had been made if Joan hadn't insisted they be informed. Naturally, the account manager protested telling the customer about it. He fretted about how to tell them and complained about having to create a plan for a mistake that would have no impact when it happened again.

Working for a Scientist like Joan, therefore, can be difficult if you don't engage fully in the Scientist's theories and systems. Engaging fully can be intellectually stimulating; a manager like Joan will be more than happy to school you in these theories and systems and will enjoy discussing them. Making the commitment to grasp the Scientist's concepts and embracing the learning that comes with it makes working for the Scientist a more rewarding experience.

TRY TO IMPOSE SOME ORDER AND DISCIPLINE

While a Scientist will fight you if you go against his doctrine, he may be amenable to direct reports who help keep the group running smoothly. Scientists often recognize that they can become distracted, fail to establish efficient procedures, and so on. If you're an organized person who can't stand sloppy execution, this can drive you a little crazy. As I noted earlier, meetings run by Scientists tend to be overlong at best and chaotic at worst.

You can make your life easier and help the Scientist by volunteering to create some policies and processes that facilitate workflow. If this is your strength, the Scientist will appreciate you putting it to work for the group. More important, though, is that you'll have some control over the Scientist-produced delays and tangents that make work life difficult to tolerate.

BE A TRANSLATOR

As brilliant as the Scientist might be, he may not be brilliant at articulating his higher-level concepts, or he may articulate them in ways that are so erudite or theoretical that his words don't connect with listeners. You end up being on the receiving end of complaints from customers, bosses, and other stakeholders who tell you they can't make heads or tails of what the Scientist just said.

As a translator, you can become adept at explaining what a Scientist believes about how a process or strategy should work in a way that gets through to a broad range of people. Being able to summarize a long-winded speech or a meandering explanation will make your job easier. You will no longer dread it when someone walks into your office with a bewildered expression on her face and asks, "What did he just say?"

PROFESSIONAL TACTICS: HOW TO WORK EFFECTIVELY FOR A SCIENTIST BOSS

One of the trickiest professional issues involved in working for a Scientist is how to maintain your loyalty to him while also staying connected to the rest of the organization. This balancing act comes into play when the Scientist is following his own doctrinaire approach and it is causing tension with others in the organization. This is not an infrequent occurrence, since the Scientist often creates some jealousy among other managers because of his theories and aggressiveness in espousing them. Other managers feel they aren't viewed by management as the Scientist's intellectual equal, and they resent it.

For someone who works for a Scientist, the issue becomes one of not burning bridges. While the Scientist may have no problems letting another manager know he thinks his approach is ill conceived, this is a luxury his direct reports can ill afford. Therefore, the first tactic is as follows:

FIND THE BALANCE POINT BETWEEN LOYALTY TO THE SCIENTIST AND LOYALTY TO THE REST OF THE ORGANIZATION

Implementing this tactic involves supporting your boss in executing his strategies and policies, but it also means forming relationships with those outside of your boss's circle who may not agree with his approach. Typically, Scientists have a circle of true believers throughout the company—it may include everyone from the CEO to other group heads. Invariably, however, opposition arises, and some of that opposition can wield significant power and is just waiting for the moment the Scientist's theories go awry. You want to hedge your bets. The Scientist won't resent your forming relationships with influencers outside of his circle and in fact may see it as valuable—he may use you as a negotiator for resources with these "outsiders." In this way, you're not as vulnerable when the Scientist falls out of favor, and while he is in favor, you demonstrate to senior management your ability to work with a diversity of people. Another way of putting this is that you want to be seen as loyal to the Scientist, but not rabidly loyal. The acolytes tend to be clones of the Scientist and aren't taken as seriously by management as those who are able to work with him but also are independent thinkers. Invariably, those who find this balancing point not only survive when the Scientist does not but tend to be able to get more done when working with other groups, functions, and divisions.

CAPITALIZE ON THIS BOSS'S WILLINGNESS TO TALK AND LISTEN

While you're not going to change the Scientist's mind about his beliefs, you can nudge him in directions that will be better for the group and help accomplish objectives. The Scientist is a sponge for information and insight, so if you can make a point he sees as valid, he may adjust his approach. For instance, Joe the Scientist was hell-bent on being the first to market with a new technology. He was convinced that a first-to-market strategy was far more important than correcting minor quality problems. Joe's direct report recognized that Joe was going to bring the technology to market first no matter what. But through a logical, well-articulated argument, he was able to convince Joe to delay the launch a few days so the group could concentrate on eliminating one quality problem that could have serious negative ramifications if it wasn't addressed. Joe still was able to be first to market, so he was willing to adjust his timetable so he was first at a slightly slower speed than he preferred.

Similarly, take advantage of the Scientist's willingness to share ideas and information. Again, not all bosses are so free with their knowledge. You'll be able to do your job much more effectively in the Scientist's group if you're well-versed in the major points of his programs as well as the nuances.

THE SCIENTIST

If the Scientist feels you have a superior grasp of his philosophies and practices, he'll lean on you to get stuff done.

Help the Scientist with His Experiment

This may seem obvious, but notice the wording—it's not necessarily the results that count but being involved in carrying out the experiment. The Scientist needs people to bounce ideas off of. He wants someone to help him tinker with tweaking different approaches. He needs someone to travel with him to observe best practices at a company doing a similar experiment. If you can demonstrate that you're interested, involved, and useful regarding whatever pet project your Scientist is focused on, he'll view you as a valuable member of his team. He'll be more likely to confide in you and to assign you to important projects if you seem like you're a good lab assistant.

THE DON'TS: WHAT DOESN'T WORK WITH SCIENTIST BOSSES

In general, Scientists are tolerant bosses. They treat their people respectfully and have relatively few taboos. Still, the few they do have are significant, so let's examine what they are and why you should avoid these forbidden behaviors.

Don't Be Overly Emotional

Scientists are men and women of reason. They respect logical argument and facts and figures. What they don't know how to deal with are highly emotional direct reports. Anger and tears put off Scientists, who believe that their people should be in control of themselves. They will edge out people who march into their offices furious or who leave in tears. On the other hand, they prize direct reports with whom they can have serious discussions free of distracting outbursts and accusations. They want their people to be civilized, and they have no use for people who don't act that way.

DON'T BE AFRAID TO ASK FOR MORE PRECISE DIRECTION

When people who work for Scientists have problems executing, it's often because Scientists have failed to be explicit in their instructions. It's difficult to know why they are so often vague or provide incomplete information. For some Scientists, it may be a function of their distracted state of mind and their false assumption that their people know exactly what they want done. For other Scientists, it may be a kind of intellectual game—they want to see how well their people can figure out what to do when given this freedom to execute. Whatever the reason, you shouldn't be shy about asking your boss to be more precise. Most Scientists are perfectly capable of providing clearer direction, but they require prompts from their people. For instance, when they say that the project should be done "by next month at some point," ask for a specific due date. Or if they suggest that you might want to tap into some resources outside the function for help, ask who they have in mind.

DON'T ASSUME HIS SUPPORT IS UNCONDITIONAL AND UNLIMITED

Scientists do support their people, perhaps more so than the average manager. They also believe in developing strong relationships with their direct reports, which means they treat you not just as a colleague but as a friend. Because of these actions, many people believe the Scientist will support them through thick and thin, and that's not always the case.

Scientists may not display the ego or ambition of some other bosses, but don't let that fool you. The Scientist's number one priority is his theory of the case and the chance to put it into practice. He will support you as long as what you want and need doesn't get in the way of that priority. You may think you will receive the raise he promised you, but the Scientist is not going to fight for it if it's going to affect his project's funding adversely.

My point is that you should recognize that, appearances to the contrary, the support you received is conditional, not unequivocal.

CAN YOU MANAGE THIS BOSS TYPE? ASSESS YOUR OWN TOLERANCE

Not everyone flourishes in the Scientist's laboratory. If I were to make a broad statement about who does well and who doesn't, I would write that people who enjoy an intellectual challenge love working for a Scientist, while those who are highly situational in their approach become frustrated with the Scientist's firm belief in one particular system. To get a better sense of these two different reactions to the Scientist, consider Jim and Earl, who both worked for Sonia, a vice president at a major retailer. Sonia, who was in charge of purchasing for one retail division, strongly believed in cultivating diverse suppliers from around the world. She encouraged her people to develop these sources, to travel to the ends of the earth if necessary to find a low-cost, high-quality supplier.

She subscribed to an approach pioneered by her old boss at a competing retailer who now taught at a major business school. He had a formula that essentially required exploring five new sources every month on an ongoing basis to meet cost and quality requirements.

Both Jim and Earl thought Sonia's almost religious belief in her former boss's strategy bordered on the fanatical, but Jim liked that Sonia had a clear and formal system for the moves she made. He liked the fact that there was a logic to her decisions, that there was some research (conducted by her former boss) that backed up the supplier approach she advocated. Jim enjoyed working in logical, orderly environments. He had always found it uncomfortable when bosses told him, "You're on your own," or "Do what you think best." He liked rules, policies, and boundaries.

Earl, on the other hand, preferred to be given more freedom to make decisions. For instance, if he had his druthers, he never would have spent as much time as Sonia required traveling around the world researching and meeting with new suppliers. While he understood the importance of looking at fresh sources to improve the quality/price equation, he thought there were more creative ways to approach the equation. Once, he suggested to Sonia that he could do all the research necessary on suppliers sitting at his computer. Sonia told him that was unacceptable, that her belief was that you needed to meet suppliers and see their facilities firsthand before you could make a judgment about them. Earl chafed under Sonia's rigid policies and thought she treated her people as if they were competent but uncreative; he preferred bosses who were more willing to trust his ideas and judgment.

These contrasting stories should help you think about whether you're more like Jim or Earl. If you're not sure, look over the following traits of people who flourish and who suffer working for a Scientist and check the ones that apply to you.

Flourish under Scientist

- Needs a clear and unambiguous structure to get work done efficiently

- Likes to know the why behind various assigned tasks

- Appreciates the opportunity to learn a new method or approach

- Relishes working for a boss who is "smart as a whip"

- Is content being part of a larger system (rather than having the chance to create a different system)

- Enjoys hearing a boss lecture about her ideas and philosophies

- Is able to be loyal to a boss yet also establish and maintain relationships outside of the boss's sphere of influence

- Likes the process of turning theory into practice and is an efficient and effective implementer of orders

Suffer under Scientist

- Is naturally adaptable and situational, believing the best way to solve a problem or seize an opportunity depends on a given set of circumstances

- Likes a lot of freedom to carry out tasks and wants a boss who trusts his people to figure things out on their own

- Distrusts all theoretical constructs and is suspicious of models and theorems that come from academia

- Hates pedantic people and grows bored listening to people lecture about their pet theories

- Likes to find the right solution to a problem through debate and discussion, believing the ideas emerge when people battle it out

- Works best in matrix structures and likes to have more decision-making authority and opportunity to work for a variety of bosses with a variety of ideas

- Is emotive, especially in stressful situations, and gets angry, confrontational, tearful, or moody when things aren't going well

- Favored teachers in school who were clear, focused, and concise, as opposed to absentminded professors

THE SECRET STRATEGY

In certain situations, Scientists can reach senior leadership positions, including CEO, faster than other managerial types. That's because they seem to have the "secret sauce." In other words, it appears that they possess knowledge of a global business strategy, a supply chain method, an approach to growth, or a financial formula that seems capable of giving the organization a new competitive edge. As a result, they're promoted faster than their managerial colleagues. Thus, the secret strategy is:

Determine if your Scientist has the formula everyone wants.

If so, you may be able to ride his coattails to the top or at least close to it. By supporting your Scientist in the ways I discussed earlier, you can earn his respect and loyalty, and your career will benefit greatly by your association with him.

I should add, however, that not all Scientists have the right formulas. Or rather, not all their formulas are right for their particular companies, markets, or industries. I've seen bullheaded Scientists refuse to recognize the writing on the wall as they kept pushing their approaches and strategies and kept meeting resistance. You need to separate their intellectual brilliance from implementing the product of that brilliance. As smart as some Scientists are, they sometimes refuse to accept that their approach isn't viable in a given situation. If you find yourself working for such a Scientist, your secret strategy is to start forming alliances elsewhere in the organization, since your boss may quickly lose his clout and possibly even his job.

THE NAVEL

6

Challenge Your
Own Values

've saved the Navel for the last of the six managerial types for a number of reasons: These bosses are probably the most difficult for most people to work for. They come in the most varieties. And they require a bit more managing than most to make the experience satisfying from personal and professional standpoints. In other words, Navels are the most challenging of managers to write about, and I wanted to talk about them after I had described the other types so I could compare and contrast them with the Navel.

As the name implies, the Navel (i.e., navel gazer) is all about ego. As you'll recall, other managers' attitudes and actions were influenced by their egos. The Bully, certainly, has a sizable ego that causes him to respond aggressively and defensively, as situations warrant. The Star, too, wears his ego on his sleeve and loves to put on a performance.

With the Navel, though, egotism is his dominant trait. While the Star's main trait is performance and the Bully's chief characteristic is aggression, the Navel is all about a selfish satisfying of his own needs. Selfishness can make working for this boss unpleasant at best and a nightmare at worst. Unfortunately, Navels abound in organizations, especially companies that offer them opportunities to gain money, perks, power, and praise.

I realize I'm painting an unflattering portrait of the Navel, and no doubt this is due to my challenging experiences working for these types. I should add, though, that most of them are manageable. If you find yourself working for one, be aware that you can make lemonade from lemons. Don't be soured on the experience to the point that you give up and quit or just hunker down in a miserable funk. You can use this manager's ego to your advantage if you're clever and know how to deal with him.

To give you a sense of how to manage an egomaniacal boss, let me give you a glimpse of my experiences.

THE NAVEL IN ACTION

More so than with our other managerial types, it helps to know some things about this Navel's personal style. To begin with, his style was expensive. He favored ultra-luxury cars, the finest restaurants (the checks were always charged to the company), and a mistress. The Navel believed he was entitled to all this and more. At one point, he arranged for a corporate sponsorship that had little to do with its benefits for the organization and everything to do with the prestige of being associated with a particular group and the chance to hang around with celebrities. He was a bit of a peacock, strutting with his mistress on his arm and his famous pals on speed dial, wearing elegant clothes and pontificating about one subject or another, convinced his audience was hanging on his every word.

Again, I realize this is not a flattering description, so I should add that like a lot of people with oversized egos, the Navel was skilled at grabbing and holding the spotlight. He was so confident in his skills, so sure his decisions were the right ones, that his bravado inspired confidence in his abilities.

In Europe, people have stereotypical notions of Germans versus the French. The following are gross generalizations that I recognize reflect bias, but if you'll bear with me, I'll explain why I'm perpetuating these stereotypes. Germans are seen as anal-compulsive, constantly checking assumptions, studying situations, analyzing before acting. They favor intensive planning and derive satisfaction from plans that are executed properly. The French, on the other hand, favor acting on instinct. They are not big fans of planning and prefer to react to situations and adapt. They have little patience for methodical analysis and like flying by the seat of their pants.

The Navel was far more French than German in his managerial style, and this style was clearly seen when he was orchestrating a new marketing campaign for our organization. At one point, he decided he knew best how to create a television commercial as part of this campaign, even though this area was outside his expertise. He had the "brainstorm" that he might incorporate the corporate sponsor into the commercial; he would not only ingratiate himself with the celebrity spokesperson for the sponsor who would now appear in the commercial but would capitalize on the sponsor's image among our target audience. The Navel brushed aside protests from our ad agency as well as some of our internal people that this was the wrong positioning for our product. He was nothing if not confident, and he assured everyone that this was the right approach, conjuring a credible argument out of thin air. This was something the Navel did routinely.

Of course, the advertising commercial was a disaster. The celebrity spokesperson who appeared in it was the subject of a minor scandal shortly after the commercial aired, and a competitor's advertising that focused on a product comparison with our product helped them gain market share. Nonetheless, the Navel would not admit that he was wrong. He never admitted he was wrong, and I suspect he never admitted it to himself. Instead, he came up with a rationalization as to why the commercial didn't work, blaming everyone from the company that produced the commercial to the celebrity spokesperson who chose the wrong time to generate negative publicity.

Astonishingly, the Navel was able to escape censure by convincing enough people in the organization that the advertising blunder wasn't his fault. Navels may not be brilliant at business, but they are brilliant at surviving. They have an instinct for self-preservation. My boss was astute about convincing his bosses that he was the right person for the job. He had a bravado that often reassured others that he knew what he was doing. He believed so strongly in himself that direct reports and bosses believed in him too. It wasn't that he had the charisma of a Star boss or the ability to wield power like a Kaleidoscope, but he had an undeniable force to his personality that allowed him to overcome his mistakes.

First, last, and always, the Navel was a salesperson. He used the force of his personality and his extreme confidence to convince the CEO to give him carte blanche for just about every area of organizational responsibility. Working for him provided a lesson in salesmanship and its value to a career and to getting things done in a business setting. If you could help the Navel sell, you were of value to him, and life was relatively good as long as you could stomach what you were selling.

TELLING TRAITS

Because most bosses have a bit of the Navel in them, it's easy to misidentify your boss as this type after you've just experienced a scene in which he acted in a selfish or self-aggrandizing manner. With the Navel, though, pursuing his own self-interest doggedly is a defining characteristic, not an occasional occurrence. This type of manager rarely shows empathy or even asks other people questions about themselves (unless such questioning is designed to meet his own needs). Sometimes, however, Navels are skilled at acting the part of a strong, organization-first leader, and their ego-driven traits aren't as obvious as I've described.

Tammy, for instance, was the founder and head of an entrepreneurial chain of clothing boutiques. She loved publicity and was frequently interviewed by the media about fashion trends, and if you judged Tammy only by the media appearances, she would seem to be more of a Bully manager—strong-willed, highly competitive, and driven. She came across in interviews as someone who was outspoken and willing to take risks in order to grow the organization—it, rather than Tammy, came first.

Those who worked for Tammy, however, saw someone different. For one thing, she lacked the Bully's intimidating air. She didn't yell that much and had relatively good control of her temper. What she couldn't tolerate, though, was any of her people making her look bad. Once, a direct report had the temerity to disagree with a strategy Tammy had formulated during a staff meeting. The direct report was a prized new hire, recruited because of her expertise in a market that no one else in the organization possessed. No doubt, this new person assumed her expertise afforded her a degree of protection. In fact, after this public disagreement, Tammy made it clear to the new hire that she should start looking for another job. Tammy wouldn't admit to her that it was because she spoke against her in the meeting. All Tammy would say was that she realized her prized recruit was a "poor fit for our culture."

Tammy, like a lot of Navels, is so egotistical that she can't admit criticism bothers her. Instead, she finds some other reason to justify her actions. When a boss responds to criticism by punishing the criticizer severely—and doesn't admit that's why she's doing it—that's a good sign that she is a Navel. Following are some other identifying traits.

RUTHLESSNESS

The Navel is not averse to throwing people under the bus if such an action is necessary for his survival. He will do whatever is required to make sure he protects himself when something goes wrong, and he will be reluctant to share the credit when things go right. Generally, the Navel has a reputation within an organization as someone you don't want to mess with. It's not because of his power or his aggressiveness, but because he has no compunction about stepping on or over people to get what he wants. More than anything else, this ruthlessness is why many Navels achieve more than their abilities would suggest they could. While other managers often have lines they won't cross, the Navel has few if any restrictions on his behavior. This doesn't make him particularly admirable as a person, but it can help him protect himself better than others in a highly competitive corporate environment.

HIGHLY DECISIVE

The Navel makes business decisions with incredible speed and without the second guessing that characterizes many managerial choices. He also makes unilateral decisions. Rather than soliciting ideas from others and trying to arrive at consensus, he simply chooses. Many times, his people are shocked at how fast he reached a major decision and how he failed to open the matter for discussion prior to the decision being made. While many managers can be decisive, they often follow a protocol that involves soliciting ideas and information from others prior to making a decision. The Navel often decides in seeming arbitrary and solitary fashion. Sometimes, his decisiveness can be viewed as an asset, since he can acquire first-mover advantage—his decisions can appear to be bold and insightful when he turns out to be right. Sometimes, though, his decisiveness can be seen as foolhardy—he makes mistakes that could have been avoided by taking things slower and gathering more information.

HUBRIS

A number of managerial types can be afflicted by hubris, especially the Star, the Bully, and the Kaleidoscope. Most of these types, however, may stumble over their excessive pride, learn a lesson, and at least try to prevent their hubris from causing them problems in the future. The Navel can be stubbornly and even stupidly prideful and act in a way that suggests he could not possibly be wrong. People who work for Navels that fail talk about how the Navel failed, often spectacularly, because he refused to heed warnings or listen to others about his strategies or policies.

Gets Things Done

Navels are doers more than thinkers. They rarely suffer from analysis paralysis or are risk-averse. Instead, they are excellent at execution, albeit executing the wrong strategies at times. Because they have such great confidence in their own abilities and ideas, they don't hesitate to launch a program or implement a plan. They intuitively recognize what has to be done to get something off the drawing board and into practice. Impatient with people who overthink and overtalk, they are eager to set things in motion, certain that things will work out to their advantage. They're not always right, but they do have the courage of their convictions. When given an assignment, they often accomplish it in record time.

Sells Well

As I noted in the description of the Navel I worked for, he was a great salesperson. Navels have the self-confidence and the desire to be in the spotlight necessary for being strong salespeople. Listening to them, you are struck by their conviction and want to buy. Unlike the Kaleidoscope, Navels aren't putting on an act. Part of their selling power derives from their authenticity—they believe in what they're selling, and what they're selling is themselves.

INTERPERSONAL TACTICS: DEALING WITH THE NAVEL'S EGO

At some point in your career, you're going to encounter a Navel; it's a fact of corporate life. There are individuals who have ascended to positions of influence based primarily on their supreme confidence and ability to execute. Whether they're really good managers or think they're really good managers, they've convinced others in the organization of the former (because of the aforementioned selling ability) and thus have been promoted into positions of power.

Handling the oversized ego of a boss is always challenging, and I know there were times when I found it difficult to tolerate the strutting and posturing of Navel managers. I remember talking to a former colleague who was working for a competitor and had a boss who sounded like a classic Navel. This boss, who I'll refer to as Dean, was what my friend referred to as "insufferable." Dean, unlike some Navels, did occasionally solicit his people's ideas. Then he claimed them as his own. He would never give credit to his people. My friend speculated that in Dean's mind, he was the one who had made the idea work—others may have suggested it, but he was the one who shaped it and put it into action. Dean was also fond of lecturing his people; he would go on and on about a range of topics, failing to recognize that his audience had become bored or was silently seething. One time, Dean talked for 15 minutes on a subject that my friend had written a white paper about, and Dean borrowed heavily from the white paper without any acknowledgment.

My friend found that after a particularly difficult experience with Dean, he would go into a colleague's office and vent, which made him feel better. Thus, our first tactic:

PUT FRUSTRATIONS INTO WORDS

Don't internalize all the anger and frustration you feel trying to deal with a Navel who has so much time to think about himself and so little time to think about you. You're going to need a confidante to whom you can express the difficulties you're having with your boss. Venting won't resolve any of the issues, but having an outlet for your feelings is useful; airing your gripes can have a cathartic effect.

FORM A RELATIONSHIP WITH ANOTHER MANAGER FROM WHOM YOU CAN LEARN

The Navel isn't interested in helping you learn and grow, but that doesn't mean you can't find someone else in the organization to help you in this regard. When I was working for the Navel, I formed a strong relationship with a financial director who taught me a great deal and spurred my development. Because he was in the Good category, he provided a counterbalance to the Navel and made my tenure under the Navel's auspices more bearable.

ABSORB HIS APPROACH TO EXECUTION

If there's one thing the Navel can teach you, it's how to implement. Many managers are very smart, very nice people, but they lack the ability to execute. This is a big problem in organizations, in that many managers are afraid to put their necks on the line by actually launching a program or project that might fail. They know that as long as they don't put any risky projects into the pipeline, they won't risk failing. Knowing how to obtain internal resources in both formal and informal ways is a key skill, and observing the Navel can provide valuable lessons in this regard. The Navel's ability to cut through red tape and push projects forward are key competencies, and though the Navel may not be willing to talk to you about how he developed them, watching him in action can provide some instruction.

CHALLENGE YOUR OWN VALUES

This is a great experience for future managers to get their egos in check. Seeing an out-of-control ego doing damage provides a good cautionary lesson. Working for the Navel, you have the opportunity to measure your own attitudes and behaviors against your boss's. How selfish are you in your work? Are you willing to give others credit when credit is due? Are you able to be empathetic and helpful when others confide in you? Reflecting on the values that are important to you is something that Navels don't do often; use the experience of working for one to engage in this reflection in order to prepare yourself to be a strong manager.

PROFESSIONAL TACTICS: HOW TO WORK EFFECTIVELY FOR A NAVEL BOSS

As I'm sure you understand, working for Navels can be frustrating, aggravating, and confusing. At times, it may seem as if there's nothing you can do to make this a positive professional experience. I remember a colleague saying to me, "Our group is going to hit the wall at some point because of [our Navel], and there's nothing we can do to stop it."

Actually, there are things we did to delay the impact of the Navel crashing and burning because of his self-absorption, and there are things you can do.

COMMUNICATE POTENTIAL PROBLEMS WITHOUT MAKING THE NAVEL LOOK BAD OR FEEL BADLY

Admittedly, this is a fine line to walk. You need to tell your boss that his myopic focus on himself has resulted in a problem that is going to become serious unless he does something about it. How do you convey this information without assaulting his ego? One technique involves finding a fictional scapegoat. For instance: "Your new policy seems to have hit a snag because of those dumb new regulations from headquarters." The scapegoat can be individuals or organizational, a societal trend or an economic hiccup. As long as you identify a logical cause for the issues confronting your group that doesn't involve your boss, you just might get him to pay attention and do something about it before it's too late.

If necessary, fall on the sword yourself. Explain to your boss that it was your mistake—that you should have seen the trend coming or warned him earlier about the quality issue. While other bosses might hold this self-admitted mistake against you, the Navel probably will forget it quickly. Because he holds everyone in lower esteem than he holds himself, he expects others to make errors. Even though it's galling to have to admit that you did something wrong when you didn't, this admission may help your boss deal with an issue before it becomes a serious problem. He may take credit in public for handling the problem effectively, but somewhere in his mind he'll recognize that you provided him with a valuable assist.

USE HIS HUNGRY EGO TO MANIPULATE HIM INTO DOING THE RIGHT THING

While flattery may not work with many managerial types, it can work with a Navel if you use it strategically. By that I mean the point isn't to butter up the boss; that will get you nothing nor improve the group's effectiveness. If, however, you can demonstrate to a Navel that a given action will result in him looking good in front of his bosses, then you may be able to help him make astute decisions.

Joe, for instance, worked for Eugene, who was a partner in a small accounting firm. Eugene had made partner in large part because he was a former IRS agent whose knowledge of the tax system and contacts within it gave him an edge on others vying for partnership status. He had assembled his group as tax specialists, and initially their clients had been companies who had or anticipated having issues with the IRS. Over time, however, their clients' concerns became broader, and they wanted Eugene and his group to handle accounting issues that required expertise they lacked. Eugene, with his ego showing, made the case that he and his people could handle any accounting matter, but he was encountering increasing dissatisfaction from clients who realized Eugene's skill base was limited. Joe, who also was an IRS specialist, talked to Eugene about the problems caused by their specialized expertise. At first, Eugene dismissed Joe's suggestion that they needed to hire some other people for the group whose skills complemented their own. Eugene didn't like the idea of sharing credit with anyone and knew he would have to acknowledge the contributions of other accountants who had complementary competencies. Joe, though, made the argument that if they recruited two or three new members of the group who had skills in areas like benefit plans and financial planning, they would earn a reputation in the firm as a "super group." As Joe put it, "No one else in the firm would be able to touch us, and this might give you a leg up on the path to managing partner." In fact, Eugene was never going to be made managing partner, but Joe's strategy was sufficiently ego-inflating that he followed Joe's suggestions.

Capitalize on Your Boss's Good Ideas

Just because someone is egotistical doesn't mean he is dumb. Navels can be very astute about business or at least possess certain abilities that allow them to be effective in their areas. Navels are often resistant to suggestions that don't allow them to shine or occupy the spotlight. A team may need to do benchmarking of best practices to improve their quality management process, but the Navel won't be particularly interested in this work if he's not a benchmarking maven. If, however, he's proficient at coming up with creative ideas to improve quality management processes, he may be enthusiastic about scheduling a brainstorming session that allows him to demonstrate this expertise.

Therefore, identify what the Navel does well, and find ways to get him to do it more. What suggestions can you make that will encourage him to make better use of his skill or knowledge? What plans can you come up with that will put him on center stage as he does what he's best at? Navels are not the most self-aware of managers (though they are the most self-obsessed). This means that they're so focused on looking good that they aren't in touch with what they're good at doing.

If you can encourage a Navel to focus more on using his business strengths, the odds are that the group will benefit because of greater effectiveness, and in the long run, the Navel will achieve his goal of looking good to his bosses.

THE DON'TS: WHAT DOESN'T WORK WITH NAVEL BOSSES

There are a lot of little don'ts that come with the territory. You have to watch your step when you're interacting with a manager who has a me-first attitude. Navels are much more sensitive to perceived slights than other bosses. They are more likely to sacrifice you rather than defend you if you make a mistake. They may lie to your face if it serves their purposes. So you don't want to drop your guard around this manager. People who do best working for Navels tend to have their antenna up; they are always conscious of their boss's egos and how that will impact their actions. They have seen how a seemingly innocuous word or deed has resulted in a Navel overreacting because of his oversensitivity. My Navel fired a direct report because of the expression on his face while the Navel was giving a talk; the Navel thought the expression was a smirk and that he was being disrespectful. I have no idea if this individual was smirking, but the point is that even if he were, most managers wouldn't consider it an offense demanding dismissal.

With this story as a cautionary flag, let me offer some other don'ts.

Don't Depend on the Navel to Advance Your Career

This point may seem obvious in light of all the other things I've written, but in the day-to-day reality of corporate life, it's easy to forget. It's especially easy to believe a Navel will support your desire to receive a promotion, be placed in a training program, or receive a specific assignment if you do a good job. For most managers, a direct report's hard, good work is often enough to merit this type of career support.

Not for Navels. There has to be something in it for them to advance your career. Perhaps if the Navel's boss expects him to develop his people and move them on to more significant assignments, he'll actively provide the support necessary for you to build your knowledge and skills and be given plum jobs. But if you do a great job for the Navel and he's aware of how much you've contributed to the success of your group, he may well conspire to keep you in place. He doesn't want to lose his most productive person and so may downplay your contributions in order to be sure you aren't promoted out of his group.

Most of the time, Navels aren't this mean-spirited. In general, they don't advance their people's careers from benign neglect rather than from some devious master plan. They just don't think about anyone's career but their own.

DON'T LET THE NAVEL MAKE YOU CYNICAL OR SELF-CENTERED

Phil's boss had managed to rise to a position of significant power and salary in a prestigious company despite his lack of interest in anything but his own advancement. "He didn't care about the team or organization," Phil said, "but because he delivered consistently strong results, leadership not only tolerated him but rewarded him handsomely." Phil asked his coach why he bothered to work so hard, to grow the people who worked for him, when it was clear that all organizations cared about was results.

While organizations do prioritize short-term results, especially in tough times, that isn't all they care about—or at least I've worked for companies that care about other things, including their people's growth and development. The danger of working for a Navel is that it can skew your view of the organization. It can make you cynical about the company's stated values and mission. It can cause you to declare that you're going to stop being a team player and start focusing on yourself.

Don't succumb to this thinking. For one thing, it's counterproductive. The majority of people who advance to leadership positions in large companies today aren't Navels. They may have sizable egos, but those egos operate within the parameters set by another managerial type. In other words, they are capable of thinking of what their people or team needs and acting on it rather than just their own particular agendas. Second, and perhaps even more important, most Navels have a limited shelf life. Their ability to generate results may sustain them for a while, but in companies that value transparency, staff development, and teamwork, they eventually fall.

Don't Fool Yourself into Believing This Is a Wasted Experience

Navels are driven. Ego is a powerful fuel, and it causes some Navels to work with great vigor and imagination in pursuit of their own goals. I'm not suggesting that you emulate the Navel but that you observe how he gets results. Hard work, energy, commitment, and motivation are qualities that Navels apply to assignments they consider meaningful. They are sometimes brilliant at locking in on the result they need to achieve and driving themselves and others to achieve it.

This is not a minor skill, so don't discount it. Instead, watch how a Navel gets things done quickly and efficiently. Their concentration and ability to prioritize in order to meet deadlines and objectives are valuable assets. Study how the Navel does it, and apply this knowledge to the next assignment where you need to produce a strong result.

CAN YOU MANAGE THIS BOSS TYPE? ASSESS YOUR OWN TOLERANCE

When you think about it, Navels teach people a valuable managing-up lesson that applies to most managers: how to tolerate a boss's ego. Inevitably, you're going to be confronted with a boss who is overly concerned with himself and not concerned with you. If you can deal with a Navel's ego, you can deal with any manager's self-centeredness. Still, some people are inherently better able to accept the selfishness of a boss than others; they focus on doing their job well and capitalizing on the opportunities that come up and don't obsess about all the problems their boss's ego is causing. It's possible, though, that you have an extreme sensitivity to managers who put themselves high above the group and show a callousness toward others that you find obnoxious.

To figure out your tolerance level for a Navel, start out by asking yourself these questions:

- In my personal life, do I usually avoid being friends with people who are so full of themselves that they never ask me questions or listen to what I have to say?

- On at least a few occasions, have I confronted people who I felt were being overly self-absorbed and not paying attention to others?

- When I've worked for someone with a big ego in the past, have I found it difficult to restrain myself from telling him that he was being a jerk?

- Do I believe that the primary responsibility of a boss is to his group or team?

THE NAVEL

- Have I ever found myself unable to work productively with someone because he was so full of himself?

- Would I prefer to work for someone who yelled and screamed at me frequently instead of someone who was so self-consumed that he barely acknowledged my existence?

Admittedly, most people answer yes to at least some of these questions. It may be, however, that your ability to work for a Navel depends on the tradeoffs you're willing to make to tolerate his self-absorption. Consider whether you would be willing to make the following tradeoffs:

- Being left alone to do work in the way I want versus being treated with indifference.

- Having the chance to get things done and make things happen versus having my contributions ignored or downplayed.

- Pursuing opportunities to acquire knowledge and skills on my own versus being mentored and taught the knowledge and skills.

- Forming supportive alliances with influential people in the company outside my group versus receiving support from my boss.

- Learning how to take charge of my own growth and development versus having someone else in charge of it.

These tradeoffs are palatable to some and intolerable to others. If they're intolerable for you, look for ways to escape from the Navel's group as soon as possible.

THE SECRET STRATEGY

Navels are not shy, especially when it comes to talking about themselves. They like telling war stories that cast them in a favorable light. They enjoy telling you how they solved a particularly difficult problem. They are quick to point out what they did in similar situations. Unlike some bosses who don't want you to get to know them or are miserly with information about themselves, the Navel will gladly tell you his life story. As difficult as it may be listening to the Navel go on ad infinitum about himself, recognize his self-disclosure is an opportunity for you to do a better job of managing up. More specifically, use this secret strategy:

View a Navel as a therapist would.

Pay attention to what your boss says about himself. Relatively quickly, he'll reveal what his biggest fears are, what he derives the most satisfaction from, who his enemies are, and what he hopes to achieve in work and in life. A treasure trove of information will drop at your feet, but to make use of it, you need to put on your therapist's cap and analyze what it is he's telling you.

For instance, Ginny was recruited to work for the brilliant head of a large company's IT department. Harold was off-the-charts smart and knew it, and his arrogance was tolerated only because he did an excellent job of keeping the company's tech systems running smoothly. The company had hired Ginny, a recent college graduate with a computer science degree, in large part because she seemed not only technologically qualified for an entry-level IT position but she was a good communicator. Harold's bosses assumed that

Ginny would be a good go-between, helping improve communications with other functions.

For the first month or so, Ginny struggled with Harold much as other employees did. His ego needed constant stroking, and he displayed no interest in Ginny or in helping her get her footing in the company. If she asked him a question, he'd just roll his eyes as if she had asked the dumbest question he had ever heard. At times, he would lecture her about what she was doing wrong and how her actions reflected poorly on him. Ginny, though, paid attention to what he said and observed what he did—she had high emotional intelligence and relatively quickly she got what Harold was all about. By paying close attention to who Harold was, she figured out how to handle him effectively.

For instance, she noticed that he was at his most egomaniacal early in the day—he needed to get a few things implemented before he relaxed a bit and became less overbearing. She also discovered that making a positive remark about something he had accomplished also put him in a better mood and increased the odds that he would be helpful. Ginny found that you didn't have to be sycophantic as much as just say something nice or pleasant about some work he had done or supervised.

In short, she analyzed him perceptively and figured out what made him tick—at least in a business sense.

You can do the same thing with most Navels. They'll provide you with plenty of material for analysis, and it will help you plot a strategy around this manager's large ego in order to keep the relationship relatively pleasant and productive.

SITUATIONAL MANAGEMENT

Tailoring Your Boss

Management to Events,

Moods, and Other Matters

All the advice in the previous pages is valid in most situations. Yet in certain situations, you need to fine-tune that advice. How you deal with a Bully who is confronted by a stressful situation like a 15 percent staff reduction is different from how you deal with a Scientist facing the same situation. You need to be aware of how a specific boss type handles these challenging situations and then adjust your standard approach accordingly. It's not that you completely change the way you manage your Bully manager, for instance, but that you customize your behaviors in anticipation of how the Bully reacts to this situation.

Similarly, you may wonder about the best way to manage your boss under what I like to think of as "special circumstances"—when you want to ask for a promotion, or when you are trying to help your boss adapt to significant organizational change. While the earlier suggestions are useful in this regard, I'd like to offer some additional advice that will provide more specific detail about how to deal with the Good boss when you are asking her to recommend you for a position that just opened up or assisting a Scientist manager who is fed up with bureaucratic red tape that is hampering his plans.

Think of this chapter, then, as providing you with more situational focus on how to handle your boss when certain situations, events, problems, or opportunities occur.

A CRISIS SITUATION

For our purposes here, a crisis is any situation that places intense pressure on your boss and your group. It can involve a demand from management that the group solve a difficult problem or meet ambitious objectives for the quarter; it can be related to a product recall or other quality issue; it may entail your group's involvement in a legal matter, such as an employee discrimination lawsuit; or it can have to do with an economic downturn and a need to boost results or cut costs.

Whatever constitutes the crisis, it has different effects on different bosses. The Navel will make decisions to resolve the crisis based on preserving his image first, while the Good will handle it with kid gloves, fearing making a mistake that might turn a stressful situation into an even worse one. Understanding how your particular boss will respond to a crisis gives you an advantage in helping him work through it, and you can earn a great deal of respect and career points by making the right moves for your type of manager.

Let's look at how each of our six respond to crisis situations, and how you should respond to them.

THE BULLY

Bullies, as you'll recall, hate surprises, and crises usually come with an element of surprise. Just as significantly, Bullies also don't like to feel as if they're not in control—or that others perceive they're not in control—and emergency situations foster this feeling and perception. I should add that at times Bullies can make a problematic situation appear like a crisis even though it's not nearly at that level of difficulty. They do so because it allows them to brag or to demonstrate their ability to management. On more than one occasion, I saw a Bully manager essentially kill a mouse and call it an elephant. For instance, an HR guy was able to negotiate a settlement with the union and promoted his ability to deal with a threatened strike, though in fact it was a cordial negotiation and a strike was never mentioned.

During a crisis, Bullies are often even more judgmental and willing to find scapegoats than normal. If you contributed to the crisis in any way, be aware that the Bully may target you for punishment. Muster a strong defense or influential allies in the organization so you don't receive the lion's share of the blame. Recognize, too, that Bullies will respond to crises with a show of strength. Typically, this means assembling a team and taking decisive action to resolve the problem. Make yourself a member of the team; support the Bully's effort to deal with the emergency. Bullies are actually quite good in difficult situations, since they aren't afraid to make bold moves. Take advantage of your Bully's decisiveness and be seen as someone who works well in challenging situations.

THE GOOD

Crises throw Good managers into a tizzy. They dislike risk, and taking some risks is often necessary to resolve a crisis. Unlike the Bully, they often move slowly and cautiously when a big problem hits, gathering information, sounding out experts, holding meetings. They yearn for consensus before taking action, and it's possible that a crisis can spiral out of control while they're trying to get everyone to agree on a plan of action. Many times, the Good's strategy to deal with a crisis is to spread responsibility around so that if the crisis goes from bad to worse, the blame will also be spread.

You can contribute to the Good's and your own standing in the organization if you recognize when she's taking too long to respond to a crisis and spur her to take action. Many times, the Good needs someone to whisper in her ear that she can no longer postpone acting—that if she waits any longer, she is taking the biggest risk of all. In addition, try and help the Good figure out what the right thing to do is when an emergency looms. By gathering data, analyzing it, and recommending a course of action, you do a great service to the Good and your group—you're essentially doing what your boss should do, and though she may take credit, she may also spread that credit around. At the very least, she will be grateful if you can help her navigate the crisis effectively.

THE KALEIDOSCOPE

In many instances, Kaleidoscopes are well-equipped to deal with crises effectively. This is due in part to their ability to avoid crises in the first place. Remember that K's are all about power, and for them, knowledge is power. As a result, they usually have the information necessary to prevent a crisis or at least to nip it in the bud. When the K's power is threatened by a crisis, he will shift into whatever persona is necessary to help him prevent or minimize the loss of power. If necessary, he will be a negotiator and consensus builder if that's what's needed to handle the emergency and keep his position and his group intact. On the other hand, he can shift to dictator mode if he believes he needs to seize control and issue orders in order to salvage what he can from the situation.

Managing this manager during times of stress and chaos can be difficult, since Kaleidoscopes will do what they need to preserve their power, and if you are in their way, there's not much you can do about it—they will sacrifice you without a second thought in these instances. Fortunately, most of the time the choice isn't so extreme. During a crisis, Kaleidoscope bosses frequently rely on the people who have the best sources of information. They want the latest news on the strike negotiations, a competitor's evolving, dominant technology, the proposed merger, the governmental regulatory action against the company, the downsizing rumor. Therefore, develop your networks broadly and deeply, make sure to check these networks regularly, and pass on what you learn to your boss. In this way, you create value for yourself during a crisis.

THE STAR

Cindy, a vice president of marketing in a telecommunications company, provides a good example of how Stars respond to crisis. Cindy's group came under tremendous pressure to create buzz around the company's new cell phone introduction. Earlier in the year, a competitor had introduced a phone and taken market share from Cindy's company. A great deal was riding on this introduction, with management communicating that if it was not successful, the company would be forced to trim staff and cut other expenses.

Most of our other managerial types would have responded to this situation with some form of difficult or even dysfunctional behavior. Cindy, on the other hand, was more herself than ever before. In other words, she loved the way the crisis thrust her into the spotlight and the chance to give dramatic, motivational talks, to be interviewed by the media, and to have the CEO calling her frequently about her advertising, public relations, and promotional plans for the phone's launch. Her people loved working for her during this intense period because she was on top of her game, making it fun and challenging to be on her team.

Stars need their people to follow their lead during crises, so take your cue from your boss. Your goal is to make your Star look good as the problems unfold, and one of the best tactics you can use is the one we noted in the Star chapter: be a good listener. Pay attention to what she says she requires. Don't make assumptions, since business-as-normal is suspended during these stress-filled times. What you used to do in your job during periods of normalcy may not be what you have to do now. Stars are good communicators, but remember that they're often in constant motion during crises, so you have to listen hard to what they say and sometimes read between the lines when they don't have the time to go into detail. Second, be quick about responding to their requirements. Stars are impatient, and they're more impatient than usual when things are hectic and pressurized. Don't be slow and methodical. Instead, recognize that Stars want action rather than excuses or data, so make execution your priority during crises.

THE SCIENTIST

It's not that an emergency throws these managers for a loop. Scientists can deal effectively with crisis, especially if they can bring their considerable intellects to bear on whatever the problem is and solve it through analysis. Many times, however, a crisis exists on multiple levels. It's not just about finding a brilliant strategy to counteract the negative event, but about working effectively with other people under pressure, about communicating convincingly with outside stakeholders, about being inspirational and motivational to bring a team's full energy to bear on solving a problem. Scientists can become frustrated when a crisis calls upon them to be more than analysts and strategists; they can feel out of their depth when it requires them to stretch and use skills and approaches that feel foreign to who they are as managers.

These are the instances when you can provide crucial assistance to your boss. As you'll recall, Scientists are receptive to feedback. They need to hear certain things during a crisis that others might not be telling them. For instance, your boss may be trying to solve a quality problem or cut staff without hurting morale in a way that makes theoretical sense. In other words, he's adhering to his theory of the case, his belief that quality management requires a rigorous analysis of data or that staff reductions must be done swiftly and without explanation in order to maintain morale. When these theories aren't applicable—and when they don't work in practice—you need to tell your boss the facts. Capitalize on his willingness to listen to what you have to say, and then say what needs to be said, even if it calls the Scientist's theory into question.

THE NAVEL

As you probably could have anticipated, Navels are often at their worst when things go wrong, and crises are things going wrong in a major way. Their reflex is to blame others when this happens; they will quickly point the finger at someone else before someone can point it at them. This is ingrained behavior, and you're not going to keep any Navel from deviating from it.

What you can do, however, is help the Navel protect himself and in so doing protect the group. Help him prepare his defense to his bosses that you did all you could to prevent the crisis from happening. Gather e-mails and other written evidence that demonstrates your lack of culpability. Even if this doesn't protect him in the long run, he'll appreciate your help in doing this work.

Second, watch your back. If there was a significant failure and your team or group was responsible in some way, the Navel will search high and low for a scapegoat. Even if he was the one who deserves the blame, he will do his best to avoid it, and his strategy will be to find someone to take the fall. To stop it from being you, prepare your defense in advance. Again, printed evidence of your innocence is useful—if you can prove that you had no idea that your direct report was going to file a discrimination lawsuit or that the machinery was going to break down, then the Navel will find someone else to target.

A POSITIVE ACHIEVEMENT

Your group has met or exceeded its numbers. You have contributed to the successful completion of a task that is lauded by organizational management. Your team has won an award. Your group is responsible for bringing in a major new customer or keeping an existing client satisfied.

When enterprises or groups and individuals within these enterprises succeed, managers are usually happy, and those who work for them benefit directly or indirectly—there's money for raises, they receive praise, their boss is in a good mood, and so on. These positive moments, though, also

SITUATIONAL MANAGEMENT

represent opportunities for direct reports to take action—a window is open for people to ask for things they need (e.g., a raise or bonus, an assistant, more tech support, etc.). Let's examine how to capitalize on these moments, given the type of boss you have.

THE BULLY

The Bully lives for results. When your team scores a victory of some sort, she is going to be in as generous a mood as is possible for her. Don't expect gratitude, at least in most instances. A grudging acknowledgment of your contribution to the group's success is probably the most you can hope for. Bullies will credit their aggressive strategies for most accomplishments—they believe being decisive, fast-moving, and hard-charging is the key to achievement.

Given this, remind the Bully how you contributed to the win. This is not the manager to be humble around after an accomplishment. The Bully may resent that you're claiming credit for something she has taken credit for in the larger organizational context, but she'll respect your aggressiveness in stepping forward (assuming she agrees that you made the contribution you're asking credit for). Be aware that the Bully may not respond immediately with thanks or praise, but you've likely earned yourself a gold star in her book, for redemption later.

THE GOOD

A Good boss like Jim isn't going to go wild celebrating success—he tries to maintain an even keel, and it's rare to see him too high or too low. Yet like everyone else, he relishes accomplishment and is much more generous than the Bully in sharing credit and giving thanks. What he won't do is allow a success to change his approach to managing. He won't take advantage of a win to ask his boss for more money or resources. He won't take the initiative and talk to the group about what a great job they did. He's going to low-key it, and that can be disappointing for people used to working for Star bosses who throw parties and find other ways to celebrate after successes.

To make the most of this situation, find a way to create a low-key celebration. Maybe it's ordering in lunch or inviting everyone for drinks after work; maybe it's writing a synopsis of how the group achieved its objectives and posting in on the company Web site. Whatever it is, if you initiate this small celebration, the Good will appreciate it. More importantly, he'll remember that you cared enough to organize the celebration of the accomplishment, which counts in his book.

THE KALEIDOSCOPE

Most achievements help the K consolidate his power, so he relishes every achievement. In his arrogance and by his authority, he will take the same proprietary ownership of the success as the Bully, though he usually is more generous in appreciating his "supporting cast." Unlike the Bully, he views each success in a larger framework. He's always calculating his next step. He doesn't bask in the glow of victory for long, like the coach who as soon as he wins the title begins planning for the coming season.

The best thing you can do once a goal is achieved is help the Kaleidoscope plan his next move. Kaleidoscope bosses appreciate people who think like they do. More than that, they recognize that their power is directly related to the support they receive. If you demonstrate that you're not satisfied with small victories and have designs on larger goals—and if you can come up with ideas for achieving these larger goals—the Kaleidoscope will lean on you more and esteem you more highly.

THE STAR

Stars respond to success similarly to the way they respond to crisis; the latter gives them a chance to problem-solve in the spotlight while the former offers them the opportunity to bask in the glow of achievement. Stars, more so than Kaleidoscopes and Bullies, are not averse to spreading the credit around, as long as they are front and center. Unlike Kaleidoscopes, they have no other agendas for success other than to enjoy the moment. Typically, Stars benefit from being in the right place at the right time, depending on their people to do the hard work that results in a success. They may be the ones who close the deal or deliver the presentation or announce the new product, but they often leave the heavy lifting to their key people.

The best thing you can do in this situation is to help your boss maximize his moment in the sun. Help craft the "acceptance" speech he gives when he wins the award, or help him rehearse the conversation he's going to have with the CEO who wants him to work on a similar project in the wake of the group's success.

THE SCIENTIST

Scientists "get it." In other words, they understand how important the team was for helping reach a milestone or exceed an objective. These are extremely smart and savvy bosses about the way business works; they know that a great new product or service is almost always the result of many minds working well together; they grasp that making the group's numbers wouldn't happen if the majority of team members failed to execute their respective tasks with commitment, energy, and creativity. The Scientist I worked for would go out of his way to thank me and others for our assistance on projects. He was very specific and thoughtful in his words and deeds, and we knew that he really appreciated the particular efforts we had made.

Scientists are logical, and they recognize the logic of rewarding people who help achieve significant goals. If you work for a Scientist and he has told you how helpful you were in helping the group reach a goal, capitalize by asking for something reasonable. Again, Scientists are resolutely logical, and if you ask for something that is unreasonable, he will be disappointed in your presumption. Instead, focus on what you believe is a just reward for your efforts, and then make your case in a matter-of-fact manner.

THE NAVEL

Unlike Scientists, Navels will not respond to the logic of the situation. In the Navel's mind, you exist to make her look good. So if you approach her with a request for something because of your win, she won't get it. She won't see the logic of you showing you can handle a key assignment successfully and thus deserving a more ambitious assignment.

What a Navel does understand, however, is her desire to look good on future projects. Therefore, you can approach her and say something to the effect of: "I worked seven days a week many times last quarter to help us land the client. I know your presentation was the key, but so was my hard work. You know I'll work just as hard in the future so we get more clients like this one, but I think it's fair that I receive a bonus this year for what I contributed." This is the sort of argument a Navel gets—she gets what's in it for her if she gives you the bonus you earned.

ANGLING FOR A PROMOTION

At some point, you'll want to move out and up. You believe you deserve a promotion based on your work, and a position may open up in the organization that seems perfect for you. You want your boss to promote you or recommend you for the position (if it's not his decision to make). If you've ever asked a boss for a promotion and been turned down—as most of us have—you know the reasons commonly given for saying no:

1. "I need you where you are right now; if our results improve and the business grows, then we may need you in a position of greater responsibility."
2. "You need to make the type of splash that offers evidence that you're ready."
3. "I'll decide when you're ready to be promoted."
4. "You've developed decent expertise, but it has to be better than decent for me to consider you for that position."
5. "Why should I promote you instead of Joe or Joan?"
6. "I can't afford to take the risk right now to try and get your promotion through."

Can you guess which boss might have said a given statement for turning you down for a raise? You'll find the answers below.

BULLY

3: "I'll decide when you're ready to be promoted."

Bully managers don't like people informing them that they believe they deserve a promotion. They prefer to take the initiative and do so at a time they feel is most opportune for them (and not their direct reports). Bullies are ego-driven managers, and as such, their self-esteem is threatened when people ask to leave their groups. In the Bully's mind, the reasoning is: why would anyone want to leave my group? Bullies promote people, but they do so when it's to their advantage. For instance, if their boss expects them to grow and develop their people and measure them against this goal, then it's in their interest to promote their people when they've developed sufficiently and will do well in their new jobs.

Your approach, therefore, should be to use indirect methods to encourage your Bully to promote you. For instance, you can float a rumor (through some of your colleagues) that headhunters have contacted you and see you as highly marketable. While this tactic may entail some risk, it may also motivate him to act to protect himself—he doesn't want to look bad when you take a managerial job with a competitor. You might also capitalize on a time when you deliver excellent results and talk to someone in HR about openings in the company; you can leverage these results to interest HR in you for openings elsewhere in the company. Again, there's some risk in offending the Bully's sensitivities by doing an end run like this. If you are leveraging excellent recent performance, however, that is likely to protect you. When the Bully recognizes that he might lose you to another group, he may be incentivized to promote you himself and take credit for your rise in the company.

THE GOOD

6: "I can't afford to take the risk right now to try and get your promotion through."

Actually, the Good might not say these words—she might not admit she's risk-averse—but that is the message that comes across. Good managers are hyper-alert to any move that might jeopardize them or their teams. If, for instance, a Good feels she's on shaky ground because of a recent failure of someone she promoted, she's going to be leery of nominating you for a plum position with that failure fresh in her boss's mind. The Good boss, therefore, may not be completely honest with you about her reasons for not promoting you—she may offer a vague "the time isn't right" or suggest that you need to put in more time at your current job before you have sufficient experience to be considered for a higher-level slot.

Despite the risk that may be involved, you may be able to convince the Good to promote you, but you need to build a strong case for yourself. This type of manager responds to convincing arguments. If you can document your achievements and demonstrate why it is fair and appropriate for you to receive the promotion, this may overcome the Good's reluctance to take a risk, especially if the risk is relatively small. Enlist others in your group and in the organization to help you make your case—the Good is often swayed by the opinions of others she trusts and respects.

THE KALEIDOSCOPE

1: "I need you where you are right now; if our results improve and the business grows, then we may need you in a position of greater responsibility."

Unlike most managers, the K won't promote people to reward or motivate them. In part, Kaleidoscopes make such strong leaders because they promote based on business need. If a promotion serves his power base well, he's likely to give you the job you want. If your group is doing great and expanding, he'll promote you to make sure one of his people is in charge of the expanded area. If, however, there is no advantage to him and his authority is better maintained by keeping you in place, you won't get your promotion.

If you work for a K, bide your time. Wait for the moment when your group is doing well, when the K himself is promoted, when the company is growing. Timing is everything when you work for a Kaleidoscope. You may have done a great job, put in your time, and a slot has opened up, and for another boss, this might be enough. But the K needs to feel that a promotion will help him expand his power base. By granting your request for a promotion, he must believe at least one of the following will be true: that the promotion will give him greater control over resources; improve the group's results; impress management with his ability to develop people; or place one of his people in an area where he previously didn't have someone.

THE STAR

2: "You need to make the type of splash that offers evidence that you're ready."

Star bosses want their people to succeed. As much as they may enjoy being in the spotlight, they want to develop their own people into stars (though perhaps not quite as bright stars as they are). Given their mind-set, they want their people to follow in their footsteps. This means they want them to capture the organization's attention in bold ways. They don't want to develop colorless corporate functionaries. Instead, they hope their best people will find ways to call attention to themselves, whether by taking on a tough project and doing well with it or by working relentlessly to achieve a group goal.

Carrie, for instance, worked for a Star boss. A recent MBA graduate, she was doing well in her first job out of school—better than good, actually. For two years, she'd worked for her Star and carried out every task efficiently and effectively. She never missed a deadline or offered an excuse. She didn't complain about the travel her job required, and on a number of occasions, she'd worked on projects that had brought positive organizational attention to the Star and his team. Yet when she asked her boss if he'd recommend her for a managerial opening in another group, he told her she needed to do something to distinguish herself. She asked him what he meant, and he said, "You have to stand out rather than blend in. You have to take a risk with an idea or make a presentation that knocks everyone's socks off."

This Star's advice is similar to what I'd offer. Think about the vehicles available to you to "make a splash": a white paper, a presentation, a report, a project team. Say, write, or do something that calls attention to your ideas and abilities. Obviously, you don't want to say or do something attention-getting that's also silly or wrongheaded. You have to pick your spots. But if you're working for a Star, recognize that dramatic moves are what earns his respect, not routine competence.

THE SCIENTIST

4: "You've developed decent expertise, but it has to be better than decent for me to consider you for that position."

The criterion here is simple. Scientists promote people who exhibit the greatest skills and knowledge in their particular area. If you're in a financial group and you demonstrate that you're a whiz with accounts receivables, then you're on your way to the next, best job. Scientists esteem competency more than people or managerial skills; they believe expertise trumps everything else.

The tactic here is: get smarter and more skilled than your colleagues about your work subject. This may mean you need to invest some time in this effort—going to seminars and workshops, signing up for courses, volunteering for expertise-building and broadening assignments. But as you share and use knowledge in the Scientist's group, she'll recognize that your knowledge and skills have improved significantly. When they improve to a level with which she's satisfied, you won't have to ask for a promotion—she'll offer it to you.

THE NAVEL

5: "Why should I promote you instead of Joe or Joan?"

The Navel is always asking some form of this question, which translates into, "What's in it for me?" Navels promote only when the promotion provides them with some benefit or advantage. They aren't doing it because someone deserves it or because it will help the organization. Their concern is themselves, and people in a Navel's groups who are the best performers or the best managerial candidates often don't receive the promotion that should be theirs because they don't understand what drives the Navel.

Here are a few benefits and advantages that can accrue through a promotion:

- A reputation for being an astute developer of talent
- The creation of an alliance with another powerful person in the company (the Navel earns the gratitude of a boss who wants you, for instance)

- The likelihood that the promoted person will do the Navel a favor in the future

Focus on these and other possible wins for the Navel and make a case that if he promotes you, he will be the recipient of them.

IMPLEMENTING A RISKY BUT NECESSARY IDEA

While this situation may seem less common than the others, it's becoming a much more relevant issue today as more decisions entail more risk. People are grappling with all sorts of difficult choices that have major downsides and upsides, and they often aren't sure if it's better to play it safe and avoid the ire of their bosses or to take a chance and earn their respect and gratitude. Should they encourage their manager to recommend a strategy that might help them open a new market but also could be a costly failure? Should they ignore the deadline in order to make sure they finish the project properly? Should they challenge the boss's pet project or traditional approach because they believe that a fresh approach could be more effective?

Taking risks that pay off can cement your relationship with a boss as well as boost your career. Let's look at the best way to achieve this goal for each of our boss types, based on each of their risk mind-sets.

THE BULLY

Bully managers are natural risk-takers, and they endorse risk-taking among their people. At the same time, they hold their direct reports strictly accountable and don't want excuses about why their gambles failed. Still, they work best with people who share their aggressive attitudes toward testing new ideas and approaches, and they view those who play it safe as functionaries and nothing more.

The best risk strategy if you're working for a Bully is to weigh the possibility of trying something daring or at least new whenever you have a chance. This doesn't mean you should do it every time, but recognize that you're working for a manager who likes this type of thinking. Even if you don't take action on a risky idea, proposing it will earn you some points with the Bully. When you do take a risk, however, make sure he's aware of what you're doing. If it goes wrong, you don't want to be in the position of surprising him, since the Bully hates surprises.

THE GOOD

As I've emphasized, Good managers despise risk. They play it safe routinely, and their policy generally is that people in their group also must play it safe unless they make a strong argument for taking a gamble and discuss it with them in advance. Carl, for instance, was a young vice president in an old-line manufacturing company whose Good style fit the culture perfectly. He had a list of rules that he distributed to all the new people on his team that related to financial expenditures, presentations in meetings, interactions with customers, and so on. Carl delineated the types of behaviors and actions that he considered taboo—behaviors and actions that all involved some form of risk. For instance, one rule was that no one in Carl's group was allowed to contradict a customer; if they disagreed with something the customer proposed, they should tell Carl and he would find a way to communicate this issue to the customer in a "palatable" manner.

Clearly, if you work for a Good boss, you need to limit your risk-taking behavior. This is not the sort of manager who is receptive to wildly innovative ideas with huge upsides and significant downsides. At the same time, the Good—like every manager—wants to deliver decent results, and invariably, those results demand at least a modicum of risk. What you need to do is establish a process and procedure with your manager as to how you'll take that risk and when. It also will reassure the Good manager if you have a worst case scenario plan if the risk doesn't pay off—how you will repair the damage, how can the Good protect himself and his group, etc.

THE KALEIDOSCOPE

Ks recognize that taking reasonable risks is the way to increase their power base, so they are not risk-averse, but neither are they likely to endorse excessive or ill-conceived risk-taking behavior on the part of their people. They prefer to hear logical arguments for a gamble, and they especially like to have their people benchmark their proposed risk with examples and best practices from other companies.

Consequently, make sure you prepare an argument for your risk with ample evidence that it worked somewhere else. What did another company or individual at another organization do that is similar to what you're advocating? Why is that case comparable to yours? How is the implementation similar? How did they increase the odds that the risk would pay off? Most importantly, outline for your boss what the power payoff is. In other words, how might the risk help her increase the size or budget of her group? How might it position her for a promotion?

THE STAR

Unlike some of the other managerial types we've discussed, Stars are tolerant of their people taking a certain amount of risk. They are driven to be in the spotlight and create drama around themselves and their group, and taking chances that pay off meets this need. Stars want their people to suggest edgy ideas, to provide them with ways to make a splash within the company. While smart Stars won't want their people to do anything crazy, they do favor direct reports who think outside of the box. As they might say, they want people with guts.

Capitalize on the Star's willingness to give his people the freedom to innovate and take chances. If you've ever wanted to work for someone who will let you try new, adventuresome approaches, this is the boss who will give you this freedom. While you're always going benefit from ideas that work and suffer for ones that don't, a showy failure that causes only minimal damage won't hurt you in the Star's mind. He'll give you another chance, and he doesn't want you to become conservative just because one risk didn't pay off.

Be aware, too, that Stars often operate based on intuition. Scientist and Bully managers also rely on their instincts to a lesser extent, but Stars are the ones most likely to play hunches. They're the ones who, after they implemented a successful project that defied logic, explain why it worked by saying, "It just felt like the right thing to do." Recognize that Stars will give you a certain leeway to play your hunches, that you don't have to offer the logical argument that a Kaleidoscope manager demands. Again, hunches that don't pay off can get you in trouble with any type of manager, but at least Stars will give you the opportunity to use your instincts.

THE SCIENTIST

These managers endorse selective risk-taking. Remember, Scientists operate from a theory of the case—they rely on a particular model or system to get work done. As a result, they view risk through this model or system. If, for instance, they believe in flattening the decision-making process as much as possible to foster innovation, they will endorse risks that create additional flattening of the system. If they espouse relying on cutting edge technology, then they will embrace risks that bring this technology to bear on the issues confronting the group.

Take risks within the comfort zones of Scientists. As long as they fall within the theories and beliefs of your boss, you should receive his support. This means you need to be clear about what these theories and beliefs are. Make it your business to discover exactly what framework your Scientist operates from so you can define the types of things he'll endorse as well as frown upon. In addition, take advantage of Scientist managers' expertise when it comes to taking a risk—their superior grasp of a work area or skill set will make them a good sounding board as to whether the risk is worth taking.

THE NAVEL

Navels may fly by the seat of their pants, but they don't want their people to follow suit. In fact, they may even become upset if direct reports take a gamble and it works; they don't want to share the spotlight with others. While their egos make them confident that they can pull off difficult feats, they lack confidence that others possess this capability. And when others take risks and fail—and it reflects badly on them as managers—they are merciless. As I've noted, they will willingly sacrifice others to preserve their own self-image.

Caution is the watchword when it comes to taking risks when working for Navel managers. If you feel certain that a controversial, untraditional, or cutting edge move is necessary, talk to your boss about what she stands to gain from it. Obtaining her buy-in before you take action doesn't guarantee anything—if everything goes south, you'll probably suffer the consequences—but if it works or if it produces a marginal result, you'll probably be spared the Navel's wrath.

TWO OTHER KEY SITUATIONS

Obviously, the four situations I've discussed aren't the only ones that require specialized approaches, depending on the type of boss you have. Yet they are four of the most common situations, which is why I've singled them out. Before leaving this topic of specialized circumstances, though, I want to mention two other situations and what to do if you have a particular type of boss. I'm not going to go through all six managerial types, but instead will focus on the one or two who tend to be most reactive to these situations.

First, let's look at a situation where change is called for. Perhaps a new CEO takes over and implements major new initiatives that do everything from create new policies and procedures to remake the culture. Perhaps the company is restructured and there's a shift from a traditional hierarchy to a team-based or matrixed system. Perhaps the change is smaller scale—your group is asked to merge with another group.

Whatever the change, your job and even your career within the company can depend on how well you, your boss, and your group deal with the mandated changes. If you have a Scientist boss, you will find him receptive to incremental change but not big, immediate shifts. You can greatly facilitate his managerial adjustment to new policies and bosses by helping him break change initiatives into incremental actions. By making the adjustments small and digestible, you'll enable the Scientist to do a much better job of implementing the mandated changes.

On the other hand, if you work for a Good, expect to encounter resistance to anything that disturbs his status quo. Good bosses don't like change; they don't like to vary the way they run their groups. I've seen Good managers chafe when told they need to implement new performance review procedures, when they were instructed to switch software, and when they were asked to vary the way they ran meetings. In these instances, your best approach is to appeal to the Good's logic and common sense. If you can make a case for a change making things better in some way, you'll get the Good's attention. If you can explain how it will benefit the group and the company in terms that make sense to the Good, then you might obtain his buy-in and enlist him in the change process.

The second situation involves coping with rules and regulations. This is a constant struggle in organizations today. It may be a diversity-related mandate for team composition or a government-imposed policy on paperwork or new budgeting or promotion procedures. Whatever it is, bosses are always trying to balance following the rules with following their own ideas about the right thing to do.

Some boss types struggle with this issue more than most. The Bully, for instance, is the one most likely to break the rules out of her own hubris and aggressiveness. While some Bully managers are impossible to hold back, some will appreciate direct reports who help them recognize when violating a policy or cutting through red tape is not a good idea. If you can stop your boss from doing something foolish, she may moan and groan about it, but she may also heed your advice and thank you later (or she may not thank you, but she will recognize your value).

If your boss is a Scientist, then you may also need to help him deal with his rule-breaking reflex, though in a different way from how you might help a Bully. The Scientist is stubborn and willful, focused on his theory or model of how he feels things should be implemented. He has a strong rationale for ignoring policies and procedures, and it may be that his rationale is valid. If you believe it is, then you need to help him formulate a plan for circumventing the existing rules. This may mean doing an end run around an enforcer of rules (the head of HR, for instance) and appealing to a higher authority for dispensation. It may mean finding a way to break the rules without seeming to break them. Scientists, much more so than Bullies, break rules out of conviction and principle rather than ego and assertiveness. For this reason, they are usually more amenable to suggestions about how to appease whatever rule makers might be offended by their actions.

Now that we've gone through how to tailor your boss approach based on the situation, let's turn to how to tailor your approach if you have a boss who is significantly different from our six main types.

CHAPTER 8

MANAGING OTHER TYPES OF BOSSES

As many managerial types exist as there are people. Just as our personalities are different, so too are our managing styles. The six types I've focused on are not the only managerial profiles you'll encounter. At the same time, these types are among the most common and compelling. The odds are at one time or another, you've come in contact with at least some of the bosses we've discussed, and if you haven't, it's likely you'll find yourself working for some of them in the future.

Even if your current manager isn't one of the six types, you can use the lessons learned to help you deal effectively with the type you do have. Your manager may not be a Bully, but he may exhibit traits of a Bully at times, and you can use what that chapter suggests to handle the personal struggles you may be going through as well as to improve your working relationship with him. Similarly, your boss may not have all of the Good's characteristics. She may be less reasonable and predictable than a traditional Good manager, and she may also provide you with more challenges than the norm. Still, advice such as "widen the Good's network" will probably apply in certain situations because, like the Good, your boss tends to work within a relatively small range of people.

Therefore, what've you've learned to this point will help you manage all other types of bosses.

At the same time, a secondary layer of common boss types exists, and I would be remiss if I ignored them. They didn't make the top six for various reasons. Some tend to show up only in certain functions and so aren't relevant to those who work elsewhere. Others are likely to exist only above a certain managerial level. At the same time, we should discuss these secondary types because they are still sufficiently common that you're likely to run into at least one of them at some point in your career, and they are fascinating types, worthy of study because of their particular management styles, both good and bad.

Let's start with a boss who is cool, calm, and sometimes a bit too collected.

THE LAISSER-ALLER

Originally, I was going to call this the Laissez-Faire boss, which means "leave alone" in French, but another word from my native tongue seemed even more apt. *Laisser-aller* translates as "unchecked freedom or ease; unrestraint; looseness." In short, the Laisser-Aller boss is easygoing and undemanding. He probably most closely resembles the Good but without the Good's ability to be conscientious and do a good (if not better than good) job. He also lacks the Good's fairness and work ethic.

What the Laisser-Aller possesses is a veteran's weary-eyed experience. He has been there, done that. This manager gets how things work better than most in the organization. If you need to know the ropes, he can teach them to you—that is, if he can muster the energy to do so. I know one Laisser-Aller in a large corporation who management suspected wasn't working at full capacity, but they were loath to let him go because when the company ran into problems in certain areas, he always had the answers; his experience essentially allowed him to coast. The Laisser-Aller is the type of manager who potentially can serve a key purpose, helping younger and less experienced employees learn and grow. The problem is that the Laisser-Aller has lost some or all of his motivation and so prefers to do as little as possible.

This manager is able to get away with doing relatively little in part because of a quid pro quo arrangement with his direct reports—he doesn't demand much from them, and they in turn don't demand much from him. It's not necessarily a cynical or even an ineffective relationship. The team members respect the Laisser-Aller's experience and expertise and feel he's earned his ease; they do a good job and try to bother him as little as possible. Though team members don't receive much in the way of guidance, they are allowed to operate with relatively little supervision or interference, which some people like a lot.

The Laisser-Aller can appear in many forms. Sometimes, a more energetic, demanding manager segues into this type toward the end of his career—he retires in place and is just counting the days until he can leave. Others have the mid-career blahs and lose their initiative because of a midcareer crisis of sorts. No matter what type he is, the Laisser-Aller is able to maintain his place in the company because of his reputation and seniority and also because he used these assets to make convincing arguments to his bosses: "Based on my experience, you shouldn't increase our objectives by more than 1 or 2 percent; it's not fair to expect more of this group at this time." That argument works, at least for a while.

If you have a Laisser-Aller for a boss, here are some tactics you can use to maximize the relationship.

SET AGGRESSIVE OBJECTIVES FOR YOURSELF

Your laid-back, comfortable boss isn't going to set these objectives and help you attain them, so it's up to you. Determine what you need to learn to further your career, and figure out a way to acquire the necessary knowledge and skills. It may involve volunteering to serve on special projects outside your group or taking workshops and other training outside the organization. If you're not sure what you should be learning, find a career coach who can help guide you. Because this manager won't be making any significant demands on you, you should have stress-free time on your hands to pursue these objectives.

COLLUDE UP TO A POINT

The implicit pact between you and your Laisser-Aller may be fine for a while, but you need to monitor what's going on outside your group and how long your comfortable arrangement can continue. Is the organization experiencing financial difficulties that will likely result in pressure being put on your group for better results? Is there a new leadership team in place with a reputation for driving people hard to meet ambitious goals? Has management sent signals that your team isn't performing at the level at which it's capable? Your boss probably isn't asking herself these questions, let alone answering them. When she ignores growing pressure for better results, you can no longer keep your pleasant arrangement intact. You need to confront your manager with the evidence that things need to change. It's possible she'll respond to your raising the alarm. It's also possible she has no interest in changing and will leave the company. In either case, at least you haven't sat idly by as the group sank.

MAKE CONTINGENCY PLANS

Sooner rather than later, your Laisser-Aller will leave—voluntarily or not. Typically, what happens is that the Laisser-Aller's boss retires and is replaced by a young go-getter who demands better performance from the Laisser-Aller's group and doesn't accept the Laisser-Aller's excuses at face value. It's also possible that because of difficult economic conditions, management can no longer allow underperforming managers to remain in place. Whatever the reason, the Laisser-Aller's tenure tends to be relatively short. Therefore, plan for the day he leaves. This doesn't just mean start interviewing for jobs outside the company. Form relationships with other managers who might be willing to take you on when the Laisser-Aller leaves. Figure out who the Laisser-Aller's successor is likely to be, and determine if there's a good fit. The key is recognizing that this cozy, comfortable situation won't last forever or maybe not even until the end of the year.

THE PARENT

Years ago, when even many large companies were privately held family businesses, the patriarchal boss was common. Typically, a tradition existed in which fathers and their sons (and sometimes daughters) went into the business, and this familial tradition resulted in CEOs of companies that treated their employees like family—or at least made efforts in that direction. This patriarchal style crossed over to public companies that also claimed to treat their people like family, and it wasn't just the CEO who adopted this style but managers up and down the line. Their cultures reflected family values. While fewer patriarchal managers exist today than in the past, this style still can be found in both private and public companies. In fact, the rise of matriarchal managers has swollen the ranks of Parent bosses.

The Parent tends to flourish in cultures and in functions where relative calm exists. When pressure exists to drive for ambitious objectives, and a great deal of change and chaos exists, Parents tend to be scarce. In these instances, organizations tend to prefer bosses like Bullies, Kaleidoscopes, and even Navels who appear capable of driving people to achieve high-level goals. Yet even in organizations with cultures that esteem hard work and great commitment, Parents can emerge. Typically, they are found in the organizational backwaters— in finance or human resources, for example. They also are plentiful in companies that are doing well and have traditions of growing their own people and promoting from within.

The Parent boss provides his people with a great deal of guidance. When I was working for a Parent at the start of my career, he told me how to behave during a large corporate meeting, how to handle myself with a particular client, and what I should be careful about when I attended a particular meeting in Paris. When you're young or just joining a company, you appreciate having a Parent for a boss. You feel lost and uncertain, and a Parent can make a highly stressful situation easier to deal with. Parents are great at nurturing their direct reports, helping them learn and grow. They're always available to answer questions and offer suggestions.

When Parent bosses aren't so helpful, they become more involved in direct reports' work than seems necessary. Parents have some of the Bully and some of the Kaleidoscope in them, in that they like to tell others what to do and they like to exercise their power. This can come off as intrusive to experienced employees who may be used to having more independence. They may also find that Parents are resistant to their ideas and suggestions; they don't believe a "child" can tell them what they should do.

Maurice was the classic Parent manager. He was fiercely devoted to his people, and once when his company was experiencing financial problems, his boss told him he needed to cut his staff by 15 percent. Maurice replied, "If any of them go, I go too." Ultimately, Maurice was able to prevent the mandated layoffs, finding other ways to cut costs and save his people's jobs. Maurice, though, could be as overbearing as he was protective. He had one direct report, Sheila, who he thought of as "high potential," and he was constantly on her about ways she could improve her performance. He was much tougher on Sheila than the other people in his group, and Maurice justified his approach by saying he wanted her to be the best she could be. Sheila felt Maurice was never satisfied with how well she carried out an assignment; rather than complimenting her on a job well done, he would nitpick what she could have done better. After a year of being treated this way, Sheila resigned, saying that Maurice was "impossible to please."

If you have a Parent boss, here are some effective ways to manage him.

SET CLEAR LIMITS

In real families, it's the parents who set limits. In working relationships, however, it's the direct report who must do so. Many times, Parent bosses like Maurice don't understand that they've crossed the line; they rationalize their actions as being in the best interest of their people. While you can't take all or most authority away from a boss, you can set reasonable limits and communicate those limits. What type of behavior do you resent and feel is unhelpful? What are the actions your boss takes that strike you as nitpicky? Parents really don't realize when they've crossed the line from being concerned about their people to being overly intrusive in their work lives. If you communicate where that line is, respectfully and clearly, most Parent bosses will heed it.

COMMUNICATE WHAT YOU WANT HELP WITH

Working for a Parent can be a great opportunity for learning and growth, so take advantage of it. What does your boss know that you need to learn? How can your boss use her leverage to provide you with training, coaching, and other tools to acquire knowledge and skills? This is the rare boss who can't do enough for you, as long as the boss agrees that what you want to learn is worth learning. Use this trait by communicating what this boss can do to facilitate your business education.

THE GEEK

Many organizations have a tendency to promote highly technically proficient people into managerial positions, rewarding them for their expertise. Unfortunately, these "experts" are often inherently flawed managers. While they know their stuff better than anyone, they often are lacking when it comes to the people side of things. They may possess off-the-charts cognitive intelligence, but their emotional intelligence is not nearly as high. In many instances, these individuals come up through finance, manufacturing, or the IT functions. Some grow into their managerial roles better than others, but they all retain a preference for using their expertise over managing people.

Geek bosses are often very logical and analytical. They are excellent problem solvers when the problems involve technical issues. They are the go-to people in an organization when things break, when they crash, and when the numbers are wrong. As managers, they can do an excellent job of leading a team of like-minded geeks in pursuit of solutions. When they are heading cross-functional teams or become managers in groups where people skills are important, however, they struggle—and the people who work for them struggle even more.

Working for a Geek can be difficult if you need a boss who can do more than provide you with technical advice. If you're having problems with other people on your team, if you want your boss to be a mentor as well as a boss, or if you want to work with someone who "gets you" and tailors her management approach to who you are as an individual, then you're going to find a Geek lacking. Jason, for instance, was a marketing person who worked for one of largest companies in the world, and at one point in his career, he was placed on a cross-functional team that was empowered to help restructure the company's information systems. The organization wanted people from different disciplines on the team in order to produce a user-friendly design, and Jason was excited about the chance to do something that stretched him. The team was headed by Cliff, who had an IT background and was considered to be brilliant by organizational leaders—it made perfect sense to them that their most expert technological employee should head this particular team. While Cliff was not as myopically focused on technology as some IT people I've met, he was also not particularly sensitive to other people. From the very first team meeting, he ignored Jason's comment about how a number of people in his marketing group were frustrated by the current system because it didn't allow them to access certain customer data in a manner that was helpful. On more than one occasion, Cliff dismissed a suggestion that Jason made as being "technically naïve," or he responded with silence and just moved on to another topic. When Jason would meet with Cliff one on one, their conversations were awkward; Cliff had trouble talking to people who didn't share his interests and area of expertise. Eventually, Jason requested to be moved from the group, telling one of the company's senior executives that Cliff "has the social skills of a toad."

To avoid calling your boss a toad and to work effectively with a Geek, here are some recommendations.

TRY TO FIND AN EFFECTIVE MODE OF COMMUNICATION

You're not going to turn Geeks into sensitive souls. They are always going to struggle to connect with people who aren't just like they are. At the same time, many Geeks are aware of their limitations and know that to be effective managers, they need to find a way to communicate with their people to gain maximum commitment and productivity. Therefore, figure out how you can best get through to your Geek, and how he can best get through to you. Perhaps you'll find that e-mail and other electronic communication is the best way for you to ask your boss questions and receive the answers. Perhaps your Geek is much more communicative when he's outside the office—take him to a favorite lunch spot when you have important business issues to discuss. You will have to work harder to communicate with this type of boss, but if you can find a forum that works for both of you, that will make the relationship far better than it otherwise would be.

Capitalize on Working for an Expert

You may not learn many management or leadership skills from this boss, but you can gain invaluable knowledge by viewing yourself as an apprentice. With a Geek as your boss, you can learn from the master craftsman. While there are plenty of technical skills you can glean through observation and practice, you should also try to acquire the tacit knowledge of a Geek. As a top expert in a given area, this boss knows lots of things they don't teach in school. She understands the nuances of various processes and procedures through years of trial and error. Pay attention to the particular ways in which she handles challenging functional tasks, and be sure to ask questions. Most Geek managers like to talk about the esoterica of their specialized areas.

NUMBER 2

Unlike most of the other managerial types, this one contains a more diverse group of personalities. What unites all of them is a second banana status and mentality. In every company, you'll find Number 2s. While they are managers in charge of other people, they possess a right-hand-man mind-set that prevents them from ever being fully in charge. Instead, they are dependent on a Number 1—a CEO or any executive who wields significant influence. Number 2s can be smart, talented, and experienced, but their Achilles' heel is that they are completely dependent on a Number 1. As a result, they can't make a decision without consulting with their boss, and they don't help their own people very much unless they receive orders to do so from Number 1.

Most of these individuals began their managerial lives as some other type. They may have been a Good boss, a Navel, or a Scientist, but something happened that caused them to lose their independence and become adjuncts of their own bosses. I've seen some Number 2s whose initiative and gumption were beaten out of them by a series of setbacks; they felt they needed to glom onto a more powerful leader in order to succeed.

The most difficult aspect of working for a Number 2 is you can't trust him. He is so beholden to Number 1 that you have to take everything he says with a grain of salt. If he promises you a promotion and Number 1 says no, he won't stand up for you. In other words, your boss isn't his own man, and it can be demoralizing to work for someone who you know is just repeating the party line as handed down by his own boss.

In some instances, Number 2s are tolerable. If the Number 1 person approves of you, you can receive a great deal of responsibility, training, and opportunities. Your boss is not really your boss in these situations, but rather a mouthpiece for your "real" boss—Number 1. This can work out well if you establish a strong relationship with Number 1, as long as Number 2 doesn't feel threatened. If he does, he will work overtime to push you out of the way.

If you find yourself working for a Number 2, here are some tactics to deal with what can be a challenging boss experience.

Develop a Keen Understanding of Number 1's Values, Pet Peeves, and Preferences

This may seem odd at first, since Number 1 isn't your boss. But Number 2's values, pet peeves, and preferences are all subordinated to those of Number 1. Number 2 may prefer conservative, risk-free approaches to problems, but if Number 1 values innovative thinking, that's what's important to you. If you provide an innovative solution, Number 1 will be happy and, by extension, so will Number 2. You probably won't have as much contact with Number 1 as with Number 2, so you need to be more proactive in figuring out what makes Number 1 tick. Talk to people who have worked for him; see if your Number 2 will divulge some information. The more you know about him, the easier it will be to work for Number 2.

Don't Become a Number 3

This is a trap people who work for Number 2s can fall into easily. People naturally imitate their boss's behaviors, consciously or not. Their boss models certain ways or actions to get the job done, and their direct reports mimic at least some of these actions. If your boss is a permanent acolyte, you don't want to find yourself in the same position. Being a Number 2's favorite does your career no favors. You don't want to cast yourself in the role as right-hand man and communicate to everyone in the company that you're merely a good assistant. Instead, walk that fine line between helping your Number 2 do his job and demonstrating that you can think for yourself. At times, voice your own opinions in meetings; be willing to disagree with your boss if you genuinely don't like his strategy. As I noted, this is a fine line, and you need to be careful not to alienate a Number 2. Still, most people can walk this line if they are aware they're working for a Number 2 and refuse to allow themselves to become a Number 3.

CARVE YOUR OWN IDENTITY

This is an extension of the previous point—you won't carve your own identity if you're a Number 3—but what I'm really advocating is finding a way to distinguish yourself from not only your boss but others in your group. Everyone who works for a Number 2 is in danger of being stereotyped as an interchangeable functionary—someone who is competent but faceless. This is a certain path to career mediocrity. Therefore, figure out what your unique qualities are, and make sure the Number 1 is aware of them. Whether it's having high emotional intelligence or being brilliant with numbers or highly competent at negotiation, communicate that you possess this ability through words and actions.

THE CON ARTIST

Some people literally talk themselves into managerial positions. They may have certain skills, but they are given positions of authority largely due to their gift of gab. They are brilliant at making management believe that they are far more productive and valuable than they actually are. This is more difficult to do in technical areas where lack of expertise is apparent (e.g., manufacturing, MIS department, etc.), but in many companies, you'll find individuals who rise surprisingly high in managerial ranks whose greatest talent is self-promotion. While people in the know may recognize these are self-promoters, many others in the company believe these are highly talented individuals who deserve to be rewarded with managerial positions.

Con Artist managers are frequently charming and gracious. They don't come across as self-involved as Navels, and they can easily be mistaken for any managerial type—even Scientists, though they lack the expertise and logic of these managers. When you first meet them, you think you've found a rare perfect manager or at least a near-perfect one. They know how to con their own direct reports as well as their bosses. While these Con Artists may not tell outright lies, they will stretch the truth. Elliot, for instance, was a sales manager who was generous in giving people great leads. He'd talk about how he had grown up best friends with Joe at General Motors and how Lloyd at Ford "owes me big time for a favor I once did for him." In fact, he and Joe were only acquaintances as children, and the big favor he did Lloyd was get him and his son tickets to a minor league baseball game. Even when Elliot was caught in a stretched truth, he managed such a charming evasion—"Oh, Joe probably has forgotten how close we were that one year in sixth grade"—that you didn't think he stretched the truth on purpose. Perhaps even more important, Elliot's con artistry also worked on customers. When an account was in trouble, his salespeople would bring Elliot in to talk with them, and more often than not, he restored the relationship to its former sound footing.

Con Artist managers can be difficult to work with because you never know if they're being honest with you. After a while, you recognize that they're spinning half-truths when they promise you something, but the problem is, sometimes they'll keep the promise and sometimes they won't. It's as if Con Artists don't know themselves what is truth and what is a lie. To these managers, business is a game they enjoy playing by their own rules. They like conning people, and when they're good at it, they often get away with it for long periods of time. Until then, though, you may stay in a Con Artist's group believing her vow to make sure you get that raise, and you work for less money than you can get elsewhere because you believe what she tells you. Or you and others on your team may trust that the Con Artist really will put together a presentation that wins a choice assignment for the team, and they'll be shocked as the Con Artist pretends to be when they don't receive it.

Con Artist managers, therefore, can be equally fun and frustrating to work for, and to make the experience more fun and less frustrating, here are some tips you should consider.

OBTAIN CONFIRMATION FROM A SECOND SOURCE

This is a pain to do, but it's worth the effort if your boss is a Con Artist. When your boss makes you a promise—that you'll receive a raise if you stay until the end of the quarter, that he'll recommend you for a new team that is forming—talk to other people in your group or to employees who have worked for the Con Artist before and determine if he's made similar promises to them in the past. Be wary when people say something to the effect of, "That guy always tells his people x, and most of the time, what he really means is y." In other words, he may promise that he'll recommend you for a team, but what he'll really do is ask the team head if there are any openings for a certain type of person and then not mention you because he doesn't feel you fit well with what is required. It's a terrible feeling to be taken—especially by your own boss—so confirm before you get your hopes up or, even worse, your hopes dashed.

Ask the Right Questions

While it's important to ask the right questions of any boss, it's especially important when you're working for Con Artists. They tend to withhold information to manipulate the situation to their advantage. In other words, they don't outright lie to you, but they fail to furnish some key details. For example, the Con Artist boss is encouraging you to attend the industry trade show even though you went last year and the standard practice in your group is to rotate the attendees among various group members. Your boss, however, tells you that this year attendance constitutes a great opportunity since a senior vice president of the company is also attending, and it will give you a chance to get to know him better. What the Con Artist doesn't reveal is that this senior vice president is jetting in for an industry luncheon and jetting out right afterward, so the window of opportunity is extremely narrow.

Therefore, be prepared to ask questions that force your boss to disclose all the information. For instance: "How long is the senior vice president going to be at the trade show?"

Figure Out What the Con Is

Con Artists all have their MO (modus operandi), and if you're able to grasp what it is, you'll understand the sort of tricks this boss is likely to play on you. Alan, for instance, was a Con Artist who was the head of purchasing for a Fortune 100 company. He was good at his job, but he was even better at getting his people to do unpleasant tasks by using flattery. There was one vendor who was particularly difficult to deal with, but because their company offered the best products at the best prices, they had to deal with him. Every so often, they would need to make visits to the vendor's site, and no one wanted to go. Alan would eventually assign someone to do it by saying things like, "You know, Joe, you're really the best person on our team to handle difficult people; you really have high emotional intelligence, and I know you're swamped, but there really is no one else who can manage this guy like you can." So his con was intense flattery. Another manager's con might be to talk glowingly about a future reward that she holds out to people as a carrot in order to get them to work harder and longer than is fair. A third con might involve making people feel like they're his "favorite" when in reality he has none.

Recognizing these cons will help you avoid becoming their victims. This knowledge will prevent you from feeling manipulated and wasting your time and energy on tasks that have little or no payoff. And Con Artists, once they know you're on to them, usually won't try to fool you into doing things you otherwise wouldn't do.

OTHER TYPES, OTHER STRATEGIES

As I noted earlier, there are many other managerial types, and I don't pretend that the five secondary ones covered here and the six primary ones covered in previous chapters are all-inclusive. Many times, people have come up to me and described a boss that defied categorization. Think about the most well-known bosses, the CEOs whose names and faces are familiar to most people. What type of boss is former General Electric CEO Jack Welch, for instance? I don't know him, but from what I've heard, he has some of the Bully in him, as well as some of the Kaleidoscope, but his personality is so strong that it's difficult to put him in any managerial category. What managerial type is President Barack Obama? Maybe the

Good? Maybe a bit of the Star? Again, it's difficult to categorize him because his style is so distinctive.

My point is that you may look at your current boss, scratch your head, and wonder if there is any label you can slap on her that would be accurate. Actually, there probably is. While I can't tell you the right label for President Obama or Jack Welch, I'd bet the people who work or have worked directly for them could. In fact, the odds are they have private nicknames for them that capture their key managerial traits.

If you're struggling to label your boss so you can use that label to manage her more effectively, try listing her dominant personality traits in work settings. For instance, Mary has the following traits:

- Punctual

- Highly organized

- Detail-oriented

- Neat and tidy

- Efficient

From these traits, you might create the managerial label, the Perfectionist. Based on this label, you can ask two questions that will help you manage this boss:

- What behaviors in direct reports do Perfectionists most value?

- What behaviors in direct reports drive Perfectionists crazy?

Your answers might be that Perfectionists value people who deliver projects on time that require relatively few changes, and that what drives them crazy are slovenly work habits such as reports with misspellings or obvious inaccuracies.

From this little information, then, you have the start of a strategy to manage your boss effectively. Certainly there's more to managing a boss than this, but I wanted to give you an emergency tool in case your boss doesn't fit any of the main categories I've discussed in detail. Ideally, you can borrow some tactics that work with our other bosses by spotting similarities. You might not have a classic Good boss, for instance, but your manager possesses at least some Good traits.

BUT WHAT IF MY BOSS IS AN EXTREME TYPE?

Finally, this is a question many people wonder about. As you probably noticed, the main six boss types I've focused on are mixtures of positive and negative qualities. Even the Navel, perhaps the one with the most negative aspects, has positive qualities. Even the Kaleidoscope, perhaps one of our strongest bosses, has flaws.

But what if you have a boss who represents an extreme— extremely good or extremely bad?

In my experience, most bosses aren't representative of either extreme, just as most people aren't. Still, I know from my research that people sometimes believe they're working for the worst boss ever created—or less often, the best.

In terms of the worst, the type that keeps surfacing is the Little Tyrant. Dictatorial, imperious, self-absorbed, power-mad, and vicious, this manager somehow keeps his job despite these traits. It may be that the Little Tyrant is the big boss—he's the owner of the company or the offspring of the owner, and thus gains immunity. The Little Tyrant contains the worst aspects of the Bully, the Navel, and the Kaleidoscope and none of their redeeming features. He pushes people around, seemingly for the fun of it. He is not appreciative of good work and expects people to be grateful for working for him and the company. He is, in short, impossible to deal with.

If you work for someone who embodies these negative extremes, you shouldn't try to manage him; you should do everything in your power to escape his iron rule. Though I believe 99 percent of all bosses can be managed effectively, yours may fall within the 1 percent that cannot, and if so, find a way out.

On the other hand, if you're fortunate enough to work for someone who represents the other extreme—a boss who is wise, kind, smart, mentoring, etc.—then managing this type of boss is a pleasure. I call this ideal boss the Seventh Leader, and I would urge everyone who spots one to find a way in and reap all the benefits of working for this ideal type. How to identify the Seventh Leader, how to maximize the experience, and how to become this type of boss yourself is the subject of our final chapter.

THE SEVENTH LEADER

At least a few times in my career, I've encountered people who told me, "I have a great boss." These people don't mean that they work for someone who is brilliant or who generates incredible results. They're not referring to a leader who is on the cover of business publications because of his dynamic style and ability to generate positive publicity.

No, when they say they have a great boss, they mean something else entirely. Specifically, they believe their boss is great because he

- Encourages learning and growth as well as performance

- Holds them to a high standard of performance but helps them reach that standard

- Tailors his approach to their requirements, making adjustments based on the personality, experience, expertise, and goals of the individual direct report

- Listens and respects what they have to say

- Treats his people both as individuals and as members of a larger unit (group, team, company)

I'm introducing the notion of a great boss in this last chapter for a number of reasons. First, I want you to know what to look for in an ideal boss and recognize the tremendous opportunity if you happen to find one. Second, I'll describe how to capitalize on this opportunity—how to make the most of the experience of working for this terrific manager. Third, I want to suggest some ways for you to help your flawed bosses reach their potential.

The term I'm going to use to describe a great boss is Seventh Leader. It follows from the six common managerial types we focused on earlier. All six of them had strengths and weaknesses (though some obviously had more strengths than others). In theory, the Seventh Leader could start out as any one of the six types and evolve into the Seventh Leader, learning to manage his flaws and acquire new management skills. Even the most challenged boss, the Navel, might be able to evolve given sufficient time and self-awareness.

For our purposes here, though, the Seventh is an ideal rather than a reality—a subject I'll discuss in more detail toward the end of the chapter. It is an ideal I've aspired to as a manager and believe others aspire to as well. With that understanding, let me try to describe what this Seventh Leader would be like if she worked in a typical corporation and how she would handle everything from feedback to team management to meeting group objectives.

A PROFILE OF THE SEVENTH IN ACTION

Tim is a Seventh Leader, though you wouldn't know it by his title or by just watching him for a few minutes during the work day. He isn't the CEO or even a senior vice president; he only recently was promoted to vice president after being with his large corporation for 12 years. Management values Tim—they just named him to head a newly formed, highly diverse team of people focused on innovation strategies—but he has a lower profile than a number of other high-potential executives.

Unlike many of these executives who are Kaleidoscopes, Bullies, and Stars, Tim is more low-key in his style. When he really believes in a point of view, he's perfectly willing to take a stance and communicate his belief in no uncertain terms. Tim is also known as a listener, and if he doesn't feel strongly about a position, he is open to hearing others' points of view and changing his initial decision.

One of Tim's major strengths is how well he listens to his team. It's not that he is a passive leader of teams but that he recognizes there are times when his people are in the best position to suggest direction. He also values their feedback as much as a Scientist or a Good boss. His people know they can tell him just about anything—positive or negative—and he'll absorb and consider it seriously. Tim has as healthy an ego as anyone, and he doesn't like to hear things like "You're not thinking clearly on this matter" or "You're showing your preference for men on the team over women," but he is usually able to subordinate his ego and think objectively about feedback.

Tim isn't the smartest manager in the room, nor is he the best motivator, but what he does do better than most of his peers is adjust to changing circumstances. When a new CEO came in and put a slew of new policies and practices into place, many longtime company managers struggled with these dictates; some went along grudgingly, and others even quietly sabotaged the new procedures. Tim, however, made the effort to change and to help his people change along with him. Though he had become accustomed to the traditional way things were done in the organization, he recognized that it was important to adjust, not only for himself but for the good of his people and the organization. He was determined to give the CEO's new approach time to work, though he also decided that if it didn't work, he would leave the company rather than work in a way he didn't believe in.

This integrity, along with his authenticity, built trust. His people knew Tim talked straight. Even when he was telling someone something he didn't want to hear, Tim didn't mince words. He also was not manipulative. Tim believed he didn't need to lie to direct reports or deceive them in order to get them to work harder and more effectively. He had faith in people's ability to respond to the requirements of a given job at a given time. If they recognized that the group was in trouble and had to deliver an exceptional performance, they would put forth the effort necessary to reach that high bar.

Tim wasn't a saint. At times he could be testy, especially when there was a lot of pressure placed on him by his bosses. At times he could also lose his temper and shout, especially when one of his direct reports made the same mistake again and again. But even when he was testy or hot-tempered, his people knew that his reactions were genuine, that he wasn't trying to show how tough he was or pretending to be angrier than he was in order to coax better effort from them. As a result, people accepted Tim's shortcomings as a person because they accepted it as part of the total package, and that package was the real deal in their minds.

THE LITMUS TEST FOR THE SEVENTH

Actually, two litmus tests exist to help you determine if you're working for a Seventh Leader. They are

- Great adaptability
- A willingness and ability to learn from one's team

To see if your boss can pass the first test, ask yourself the following questions:

- Does he vary his management style based on situational need? Is he able to move from issuing orders to requesting advice and then back again?
- Does he take different managerial approaches with different people? Is he able to be empathetic with a direct report who needs empathy while being tough with someone who needs to be held accountable?
- Can he display the positive traits of at least two of the six managerial types when necessary? Is he able to be the Scientist when he must draw all the group's expertise out to deal with an issue? Can he drive results like a Bully?
- Is he appropriately adaptable? Is he able to shift to a new way of operating in order to fit the situation?
- Can he adapt without an agenda? Is his flexible approach based on solving problems or capitalizing

opportunities that benefit the group rather than on helping him achieve personal goals?

This last question is important, since it helps differentiate the Seventh Leader from a Kaleidoscope. The latter shifts personas in order to accumulate personal power. The Seventh Leader makes her shifts to help the group achieve its goals. This ability is unusual in managers. Most bosses tend to take action based on their dominant managerial mode. The Scientist, for instance, makes decisions based on his theory of the case. While there may be exceptions to this rule, the majority of the time his standard way of operating predominates. The ability to manage situationally—to free oneself from a singular way of running meetings, making decisions, giving presentations, relating to direct reports—is unusual. A boss who is able to be truly adaptable in her approach is most likely a Seventh Leader.

The second criterion involves learning from one's team. Most team or group managers believe they should teach their people rather than learn from them. Even the best Scientists, Stars, and other managerial types tend to have the attitude that they lead and their people follow. They believe that because of their "higher" title and superior experience and expertise, they should tell others what to do.

In fact, the Seventh Leader recognizes that for every ten situations, he should impose once and convince the nine other times. This Seventh Leader is sufficiently comfortable in his skin that he doesn't feel the need to impose his solutions and ideas on his direct reports in every or even in most situations. I remember this point being driven home to me when I was leading my group in a discussion of a thorny issue. Our dialogue had gone on for what seemed to me a very long time without consensus or resolution. Fed up with our conversational circles, I said, "This is over now. We'll handle the training program in the way that I think will work best." One of the senior people on my team said, "Wait a second. I don't agree. Why are you deciding that it should be done this one way?" I said, "Because I am the boss." She responded, "That's not leadership."

And she was right. Tabling debate and discussion by saying "Because I am the boss" is a red flag for a bad boss. Pulling rank means the boss is too tired, lazy, or insensitive to listen to the arguments his people want to make. As a result, they don't learn from their teams because they don't let them have their say.

Great bosses are learners. They look to learn from everything—the Internet, books, training courses, observing others and their own people. If you're looking to identify a Seventh Leader, here's a simple question:

Is she willing to admit that she doesn't know something?

Most bosses don't like to appear clueless. More to the point, they like to appear as if they know more than others. But in our fast-changing, ever-expanding world of information, this is no longer possible. Given the unpredictability and volatility of our environment, we need to depend on a range of other people to get the full story. Seventh Leaders are capable of swallowing their pride and admitting they don't understand something or don't know how to do something.

I once had a successor, a Star, who took over leadership of my group and seemed well-qualified for the job. She had an excellent track record in HR, and she had managed other teams in the past with good results. But I knew this position she was taking on was different. For a number of reasons, the team couldn't be run as she had run other teams in the past. A number of tricky HR issues existed that she had never handled before. The diverse team had also created a methodology for working together that varied from the norm.

With typical Star bravado, however, my successor ignored all these facts and imposed a process designed to get things done fast and innovatively. No doubt, this process had worked for the Star in the past, but it didn't work in this new assignment. The team tried to get across to her salient points about the HR issues they were facing and their way of operating, but she refused to listen. As a result, she foundered in this assignment, as did her people.

FEEDBACK FLOWS BOTH WAYS

Most organizations emphasize the importance of bosses providing feedback, but they usually place far less emphasis on bosses absorbing feedback from their people. I just noted that Seventh Leaders learn from their teams, and the main way in which they learn is via feedback. They encourage feedback not just from one person, but from a diverse group. They also take that feedback to heart—and to their head. In other words, they take it seriously, and they reflect on what they hear.

If you're a manager or a leader, you probably just read this paragraph and protested, "But I want feedback from my people!" Wanting it isn't the same as getting it. And receiving it isn't the same as absorbing it. And absorbing it isn't the same as doing something about it.

Think about our six managerial types and how they handle feedback.

The Bully is too busy telling other people what they need to do to pay much attention to others. She may listen to you at times, but these times are relatively rare—when she's in serious trouble and needs help, or when you possess information that she needs to accomplish a task. Most of the time, the Bully neither encourages feedback from others nor listens closely when it is offered.

The Good, on the other hand, does encourage feedback. Unfortunately, he is not particularly interested in reflecting on what it says about him as a manager. That's because doing so might necessitate facing some tough realities and making some changes. The Good likes things to go along smoothly and consistently. He isn't interested in changing how he manages and in the process raising the risk that his new approach might not work.

The Kaleidoscope is good at receiving certain types of feedback from his people—any information that helps him consolidate or build his power base is appreciated. But if you offer personal feedback—suggestions about how he might better lead the team, foster more innovation and participation, etc.—then you're likely to encounter resistance. The K feels that even constructive criticism is a challenge to his authority.

The Star loves positive feedback, but she lacks the temperament to really listen and reflect on what you're telling her. The back-and-forth of a good feedback session isn't of interest to most Stars. There's insufficient drama. Like children, they become bored easily. So while Stars may tell you they're glad to hear feedback from you, they aren't particularly skilled at using it to become better managers.

The Scientist prefers discussions that revolve around work issues. He can talk and listen for hours when the subject is his area of expertise, but he is not so open and involved when the subject is interpersonal issues. If you explain how he needs to clamp down on lax quality control during the post-production process, he'll be all ears. If you explain how his pedantic attitude is preventing many of his people from being as involved and committed to projects as they should be, your words will go in one ear and out the other.

The Navel doesn't want to hear what you have to say, and if you say it, he'll ignore it. Of all the types, Navels are the worst when it comes to absorbing feedback. By definition, some of the best feedback from a team isn't flattering—pointing out managerial flaws, missed opportunities, and mistakes provides people with the knowledge necessary to change and improve. Navels find this type of feedback threatening, so their egos won't allow it in.

Obviously, some of these types are better than others when it comes to feedback, but none of them approaches the Seventh. If anything separates the Seventh from other managerial types, it's her ability to

- Invite feedback
- Listen deeply and reflectively to what she is told
- Analyze its value objectively
- Integrate valued feedback into her managerial style, changing her behaviors as necessary

Ultimately, people who work for these feedback-friendly managers benefit in terms of their careers. That's because their groups or teams tend to perform better than others.

One of the keys to managerial performance is what Dr. Paul Hersey, a professor and author, refers to as "Situational Leadership." In my own words, they are the managers who can transition from being empathetic coaches to being brilliant implementers to being terrific motivators to being savvy negotiators, and they are the ones who lead their groups to greatness. The problem is that most managers don't recognize that they need to adjust their approach based on a changing situation—they don't see how being more nurturing or more decisive is crucial to taking advantage of a given set of circumstances. That's because they're so enmeshed in the day-to-day responsibilities of running their groups that they fail to see the larger picture. Listening to feedback from a team, however, provides the perspective that allows them to adjust to evolving situations. Everyone who is a member of a high-performing team reaps career benefits, and Seventh Leaders virtually assure this type of performance.

Second, people who work for Seventh Leaders have a chance to be far more involved in the team than individuals who work for other types of bosses. When you are encouraged to provide feedback and know your contributions will be taken seriously, you are willing to share the type of "constructive feedback" most direct reports are loath to bring up to their bosses. Fear of punishment or belief that what they have to say doesn't matter keeps them mute or causes them to say what they think their boss wants to hear. With a Seventh Leader, however, people can speak freely. This not only makes the work experience far more satisfying, but it allows them to voice opinions and ideas that actually mean something. Jose, who worked for someone who was close to the Seventh Leader ideal, said the best thing about working for his boss was that on a number of occasions when he provided feedback, his boss took notes on a yellow legal pad. "I've never had that happen before," Jose said. "And he wasn't doing it just for show. More than once, I'd tell him something, he'd write it down, and a day, a week, or a month later, I'd see evidence that he had used what I told him in some way. For probably the first time in my career, I felt like I was making a significant impact on what my group did."

THE OPPORTUNITY TO LEARN WHILE YOU EARN

Most bosses aren't consistent or effective teachers. Sometimes, if they're Navels or Bullies, they're just not that interested in passing on what they know. Sometimes, Stars and Scientists would like to share their knowledge and help their people succeed, but other matters take precedence. The Good may teach only on those occasions when other matters aren't occupying his time and attention. And the Kaleidoscope teaches when it suits his purpose—he needs to develop a right-hand man to execute specific types of assignments.

While organizations may want their managers to teach, this goal often doesn't translate into practice. Consequently, organizational knowledge is passed down sporadically at best, and people are often forced to learn on their own. Typically, bosses tell their people (or suggest it in so many words): "Do as I do." This isn't necessarily wrong—learning by doing is the classic apprentice approach to gaining knowledge—but it is also inefficient and sometimes counterproductive. People who work for "bad" bosses do as their managers do and pick up bad habits. But even people who work for the six types

I've described frequently don't maximize the learning experience. They don't grow and develop as quickly and as effectively as they should because their bosses are disinterested in teaching at least some of the time.

The Seventh Leader boss not only is eager to teach but is skilled at doing so. Early on in my career, I had a boss who taught me the importance of hard work. Joanna was a financial executive who kept talking about how the people who were diligent, industrious, and committed tended to be ones who received the best jobs, raises, and so on. She pointed out examples of people who had moved up in the company primarily because of their willingness to stay late and do what was needed to get jobs done. She also showed me that one of the best comments anyone in the company could receive on a performance review were the words, "He's a hard worker." She made this point ten different ways and it sank in.

If you can find a Seventh Leader boss, you are truly fortunate, since you're likely to acquire the knowledge and skills that will give your career a huge boost. If you find yourself working for someone who is a true teacher, capitalize by doing the following.

COMMUNICATE THAT YOU WANT TO LEARN— AND WHAT YOU WANT TO LEARN

Seventh Leaders have many skills, but they're not mind readers. If you have a manager who seems eager to teach you something, try to focus his teaching on what you believe is crucial for your development. Your boss may weigh in on what this competency is, but the key thing is to make it clear that you are eager to learn. Even Seventh Leaders aren't going to teach everyone equally—they will select those individuals who are most receptive to being taught. Therefore, make an effort to talk to your boss about areas you're interested in, skills you want to acquire or polish, and career goals you want to achieve. This will allow your boss to select assignments that will stretch you as well as provide other resources for your development. Unlike other bosses, the Seventh Leader doesn't need to be convinced to make this teaching effort— he just needs to know you're eager to learn.

VOLUNTEER

Give your boss the chance to teach in different types of forums. It's not just about sitting down with your manager and having him tell you what you need to know. It's about working with him on various assignments in different environments that will allow him to share his knowledge and further your learning and development. This means making him aware you're available for travel, to join him at the trade conference, to serve with him on a team or task force, to help him with a benchmarking expedition, and so on. Understandably, you've had managers in the past where you wanted to minimize the amount of time spent with them. When you have a manager who is eager to teach, though, you want to maximize the amount of time you spend together.

REQUEST OTHER DEVELOPMENT OPPORTUNITIES

The Seventh Leader isn't just eager to teach you; she's eager for you to learn and grow in other ways. More so than other bosses, she'll be receptive to reasonable requests that allow you to acquire work-related skills and knowledge. Unlike most other bosses, she won't resent your taking time off from your regular job to spend time in other offices or working on assignments that don't directly benefit the group. As you've probably experienced, some bosses are suspicious of requests to participate in activities that aren't focused on achieving team or group goals; they act as if you are goldbricking or just aren't interested in the tasks at hand. The Seventh Leader recognizes the long-term value of your acquisition of new knowledge and skills, and she'll accept some short-term decline in productivity. Common opportunities range from workshops to overseas assignments, and as long as your boss sees the value of learning to your career and to the group, she should have no problem helping you take advantage of these educational experiences.

FACT OR FICTION: DO SEVENTH LEADERS EXIST?

In one sense, Seventh Leaders don't exist because they're an ideal. If you're looking for a perfect boss, you have a long search in front of you. I have never found a manager who was tremendously adaptable, incredibly empathetic, a willing learner and teacher, a possessor of wisdom, and so on. Even the best bosses are flawed in some way—they're incredibly empathetic, but they are inflexible when it comes to certain issues, for instance.

Yet we need our ideals, both as direct reports and as bosses ourselves. Without a clear model for being a great boss, we don't know what to look for in a manager and we don't know how to be a good one.

It may be useful for you to know how I came up with this Seventh Leader ideal. At one point in my career, I was the head of a terrific team, one where each member was making a significant but different contribution. One team member was brilliant at resolving conflict and moving us toward consensus;

another was a great presenter who sold our ideas with élan; a third had a great understanding of human resources processes; a fourth was an aggressive, dominating implementer who made sure things were done on time and on budget. While working with them, the following thought occurred to me: "If we somehow could combine all our talents in one person, he would make a great leader."

While all these talents can't be cloned into one individual, teams can produce great leaders. In other words, a manager can learn from his team members and use their talents wisely. This manager may be a Bully, but he recognizes that he has a team member who possesses the empathy and other people skills he lacks; he uses this person as a complement to his own management style. Or the team head is a Good boss and capitalizes on the Bully who is a member of his team to push the team's agenda forward.

This Seventh Leader, then, displays the two traits that I suggested were the litmus test for this ideal type: adaptability and an ability to learn from his team.

This type of boss does exist. I suspect that at one point in your career, you worked for a manager who may not have been the smartest person in the room or had the highest emotional intelligence, but she was highly situational and highly receptive to her team's suggestions. She elevated herself above the boss norm with these two qualities, and I would bet superior team performance was the result.

Finding these bosses and finding ways to work for them should be your goal. In the coming days, weeks, and months, they will provide a degree of safety in the storm. As organizations continue to downsize, struggle with competitive threats from China, India, and elsewhere, and attempt to deal with issues such diversity and being green, the need for outstanding bosses will be greater than ever before. People who work for these bosses will enjoy a degree of protection they otherwise wouldn't have working for other managers. Companies will come to esteem Seventh Leader types, recognizing that their flexibility and ability to learn from teams makes them significant contributors to the company. They'll be able to keep their people committed and energized even during morale-lowering cycles. They'll be able to get the maximum performance from their team members because they know how to adjust their style so they bring people together during tough times. In a volatile business environment, Seventh Leaders are able to respond to that environment and manage appropriately rather than stick to a one-note style.

I should add that if you find this type of boss, you'll find him relatively easy to manage. In a sense, Seventh Leaders manage themselves. You don't have to strategize the best ways to keep them happy, out of your hair, networked, or focused on team goals because they are motivated to do these things on their own—and if they can't, they're perfectly willing to ask team members or other organizational employees for help. Thus, you can focus on doing your job and being as productive as possible rather than wasting time and energy trying to cope with your boss's idiosyncrasies and dysfunctions.

HELP YOUR BOSSES
REACH THEIR POTENTIAL

Most people assume that their boss is there to help them reach their potential. While that certainly is a charge of a good boss, I'm suggesting that it's also the responsibility of a good direct report. The more you can help your Bully, Good, Kaleidoscope, Star, Scientist, or Navel manager move toward the Seventh ideal, the better off you'll be. Not only will your boss be grateful for how you're helping him increase his managerial effectiveness, but as this manager takes on at least some Seventh Leader traits, your entire group will benefit, becoming a much more productive unit with higher morale.

If you are currently working for a Navel, or you are down on your boss for other reasons, it may seem far-fetched to think he can approach any sort of ideal status. This may be true. Some bosses are doomed to be mediocre or worse forever, and if you work for this type, your best strategy is to find a way out as soon as it's feasible.

My experience convinces me, however, that the majority of managers can improve no matter what their type might be, and they can acquire some Seventh Leader attributes. With that optimistic thought in mind, let me take you through each of our six types and suggest what you might do to move them toward Seventh status.

THE BULLY

The biggest challenge for the Bully is learning from a team. While Bullies are capable of adjusting to shifting circumstances (though they may adjust fast and furiously, as is their nature), they often place undue faith in their own capacity to figure out solutions to problems. They believe they must be in charge, that they are the ones who have to issue orders and set direction. They believe this even when they lack the skills, knowledge, or temperament for handling a given person or situation effectively.

If you have a boss like this, one way to get him to start listening to his team is by mentioning a given team member's knowledge or expertise in relation to a particular issue the team is facing. You don't want to be overly direct; the Bully will react defensively if he believes you're suggesting he can't handle something himself. Instead, reference this expertise casually: "Did you know that when John worked at General Motors, he contributed to the design of their antilock brakes?" or "I was talking to Mary the other day, and I was surprised when she told me that she ran a diversity program a few years back like the one the CEO is trying to get going." If the Bully is smart, he'll pick up on these cues, start listening and learning from his team members, and, if their ideas pan out, be more proactive in learning from them in the future.

The Good

Good bosses need to aim higher if they want to be like Seventh Leaders. Too often, they settle for safe solutions and competence, for rituals and routines. They don't like changing their approach because it entails risk, even if there is a significant reward for doing things differently.

Admittedly, it's tough to move Good bosses away from their standard operating procedure. But if Good managers recognize that there's more risk to maintaining the status quo than to changing, they might make the necessary adjustments as a Seventh Leader would. Therefore, communicate the risks of adhering to business-as-usual processes and policies. Give them examples of how other people who stubbornly stuck to certain practices paid a stiff price because of their inability to adjust. Use examples from your company if possible, but ones from other companies in other industries are fine. Suggest that the real risk is in maintaining performance rather than changing strategy and seeking improved results. If the Good sees risk in the status quo and safety in a higher level of performance, he may be motivated to adapt.

THE KALEIDOSCOPE

Of all the six types, the K probably has the greatest potential as a Seventh Leader, if for no other reason than her understanding and use of power. She is willing to learn from her team and adapt to circumstances if it allows her to consolidate her power. This is all the incentive she needs to manage situationally and to involve her people in the decision-making process.

What militates against her doing so, however, is if she becomes convinced that these actions will somehow diminish her as a manager and as a leader. Some Ks are fearful to the point of paranoia that others are chipping away at their authority. They become rigid and unwilling to listen to others when this fear is sufficiently strong. Your goal, therefore, is to assuage this fear. Make an argument for how being flexible in a certain situation or leaning heavily on the team will result in greater power for the K in the long term. She will be willing to accept some short-term diminution of her authority if she feels that her position will be strengthened in the long term.

THE STAR

Stars will never achieve or even approach Seventh Leader levels unless they are willing to share the spotlight with their teams. Too often, they are so fixated on the drama of being a manager and being the person around whom the drama unfolds that they see their team as a supporting cast. Seventh Leaders treat their people as equals. Though the Seventh is in charge, he never presumes that he is somehow superior except in title and position power. By valuing his people, he gives them the confidence to make suggestions and try out new concepts.

To help Stars become more responsive to their teams, create a spotlight strategy that involves team members. Perhaps one individual has an idea for a new product that might revolutionize the category. Perhaps another team member wants to write a provocative white paper. You might propose the group restructure in a way the company has never tried before. Helping Stars see the dramatic possibilities of ideas and actions of team members changes their perspective on listening and learning from team members. When they see how it can help the spotlight shine brighter, they don't mind as much sharing it with others.

THE SCIENTIST

What makes Scientists such strong managers are their deeply held beliefs and theories—they are sure about what works and use their high level of expertise to achieve significant objectives. Their knowledge and the way they frame it can be impressive, carving out a niche for them in the company. Yet the almost religious fervor they bring to their management theories and other systems can work against them, at least from a Seventh Leader perspective. They are not adaptable because of their beliefs—they know only one way of approaching problems and opportunities.

While you're not going to get a Scientist to give up his theory of the case, you can get him to add corollaries and exceptions to the rule that make him a little more adaptable as a manager. For instance, your Scientist believes in "first mover theory"—that the first one into a market tends to be the winner. Because of this belief, he's rushing your group to develop a new product and introduce it at a very fast pace—too fast, you and other group members believe, for the product to be developed without the risk of significant bugs. Rather than challenge the Scientist's first mover theory, you agree with it but suggest that this particular product and market are an exception to the rule. You create a corollary theory that posits that first mover works except when the pace of development is so fast that significant quality problems are likely. By using the Scientist's pet theory, you increase the odds that he'll listen and adjust.

THE NAVEL

Yes, it's possible for Navels to acquire some qualities of Seventh Leaders, but they do have the furthest distance to travel to get them. Because of their large egos and self-absorption, they pay scant attention to their people and are inflexible. Their hubris blinds them to the mistakes they're making and the need to admit a mistake and rethink premises.

Some Navels, however, are damaged managers, and some of the damage can be undone. It's likely that in the past, they were "abused" by their bosses—yelled at, criticized unmercifully, scapegoated—and they reacted by inflating their egos as a defense mechanism. When they became managers, they kept these inflated egos intact.

You may be able to undo some of this damage by serving as the Navel's confidante. Some Navel bosses need to vent, to express their fears and frustrations, to explain why they're so self-protective. These conversations need to take place over time—enough time so that you can earn the Navel's trust. In some instances, having a confidante provides the Navel with enough support that her ego doesn't need constant stroking.

She'll start listening to the confidante, and the confidante can suggest she listen to other members of the group.

I don't want to appear a Pollyanna and tell you that most or even the majority of Navels can become Seventh Leaders. I would be the last one to tell you to try any of these tactics on a boss you feel is never going to change one iota.

Use your intuition when it comes to assessing if your boss has Seventh Leader potential. If you've worked for a manager for a while, you probably have a good sense of whether he is completely locked in to who he has been as a boss or whether there's room for change and growth. If so, then you may want to see if you can help these people become the best bosses you've ever had.

This doesn't mean you're going to change them into someone different. The Bully is always going to be determinedly aggressive; the Star is always going to love the drama of work. Even the secondary tier of boss types we examined in Chapter 8—the Geek, the Con Artist, the Number 2, etc.— are going to retain their essential qualities no matter how well their direct reports are able to manage them.

So as you go forth and attempt to manage your managers, keep in mind that the goal is not to change people into something they're not and never can be. Instead, it's to help them reach their potential as bosses. If you can do that, you'll discover that you haven't just helped your manager, but you've helped yourself.

INDEX

Bully manager *(Continued)*:
    biggest challenge for, 209
    crisis situation, 143–144
    the Don'ts, 18–21
    feedback process, 200
    identification questions, 6–9
    interpersonal tactics, 9–14
    positive achievement, 150
    potential to become Seventh Leader, 209–210
    professional tactics, 14–17
    risky-but-needed decisions, 160–161
    rules and regulations, 167
    secret strategy, 24–25
    telling traits, 6–9
    tolerance assessment, 21–23

C

Calculating behavior *(See* Manipulative and calculating behavior)
Calm behavior:
    with Bully manager, 25
    of Good manager, 27–49
Calm setting, Parent manager in, 175
Career advancement, with Navel manager, 134–135
Challenging projects, with Good manager, 36–37, 42–43
Chameleon *(See* Kaleidoscope manager)
Change, dealing with, 106–107, 166
Charismatic, Star manager as, 73–95
Charming:
    Con Artist manager as, 184
    Kaleidoscope manager as, 54
Coasting, by Laisser-Aller manager, 171–174
Collusion, with Laisser-Aller manager, 173–174
Communication:
    with Bully manager, 25
    with Geek manager, 179–180
    and learning, with Seventh Leader, 204–205
    to Navel manager, 128–131
    with Parent manager, 177
    (See also specific topics)

Compassion and empathy:
    by Navel manager, 124
    by Star manager, 76–77
Competence, of Good manager, 29–34
Competitiveness, of Bully manager, 3–5
Con Artist manager, 183–187
Confidence:
    of Bully manager, 4, 6
    of Navel manager, 121–122, 128
    of Star manager, 78–79
Confirming Con Artist information, 185
Confrontation, by Good manager, 30–31
"Cons," identifying, of Con Artist manager, 186–187
Consistency, of Good manager, 43–44
Contingency plans, with Laisser-Aller manager, 174
Control and steering, of Star manager, 83–85
Crisis situation:
    Bully manager, 4, 143–144
    Good manager, 144–145
    Kaleidoscope manager, 145–146
    Navel manager, 148–149
    Scientist manager, 147–148
    Star manager, 146–147
Crusading approach, by Star manager, 76
Cynicism, and Navel manager, 135–136

D

Day-to-day interactions:
    Bully manager, 1–25
    Con Artist manager, 183–187
    facilitation benefits, xxviii
    Geek manager, 177–180
    Good manager, 27–49
    Kaleidoscope manager, 51–72
    Laisser-Aller manager, 171–174
    Little Tyrant, 189–190
    Navel manager, 119–140
    Number 2 manager, 180–183
    Parent manager, 174–177
    Perfectionist manager, 188–189

Good manager *(Continued)*:
    crisis situation, 144–145
    the Don'ts, 42–44
    feedback process, 200
    identification questions, 32–34
    interpersonal tactics, 35–37
    positive achievement, 150–151
    potential to become Seventh Leader,
        210–211
    professional tactics, 37–42
    risky-but-needed decisions, 161–162
    secret strategy, 49
    telling traits, 32–34
    tolerance assessment, 44–48
"Good soldier," to Star manager, 91

H

Hersey, Paul, 202
Hidden agenda, Kaleidoscope
    manager, 68
Hubris, of Navel manager, 126
Humor, finding, and Bully manager,
    12–13

I

Ideal, Seventh Leader as, 193, 208–214
Idealistic people, and Bully manager,
    5
Identification questions:
    Bully manager, 6–9
    Good manager, 32–34
    Kaleidoscope manager, 57–59
    Navel manager, 124–127
    Perfectionist manager, 188–189
    Scientist manager, 103–106
    Seventh Leader, 196–199
    Star manager, 79–82
Identity building, with Number 2
    manager, 183
Implementation, by Navel manager,
    129
Implementers, Star manager as, 79–80
Impulsiveness, of Star manager, 73–95
Information:
    conveyed, by Scientist manager,
        101

source of:
    to Bully manager, 15–16
    to Kaleidoscope manager, 64–65
Inside knowledge, of Kaleidoscope
    manager, 65–66
Intellectual approach, of Scientist
    manager, 98–118
Intelligence, of Kaleidoscope manager,
    51–72
Interpersonal tactics:
    Bully manager, 9–14
    Con Artist manager, 185–187
    Geek manager, 179–180
    Good manager, 35–37
    Kaleidoscope manager, 60–63
    Laisser-Aller manager, 173–174
    Navel manager, 127–130
    Number 2 manager, 182–183
    Parent manager, 176–177
    Scientist manager, 106–109
    Star manager, 82–85
Intimidation, by Bully manager, 3–6

K

Kaleidoscope manager, 51–72
    action and behavior, 53–57
    asking for promotion, 156–157
    becoming the Seventh Leader, 211
    biggest challenge for, 211
    crisis situation, 145–146
    the Don'ts, 66–68
    feedback process, 200
    identification questions, 57–59
    interpersonal tactics, 60–63
    positive achievement, 151–152
    potential to become Seventh Leader,
        211
    professional tactics, 63–66
    risky-but-needed decisions, 162
    secret strategy, 71–72
    telling traits, 57–59
    tolerance assessment, 69–70

L

Laisser-Aller manager, 171–174
Learners, Seventh Leader as, 198

Learning:
from Geek manager, 180
from Seventh Leader, 203–206
Life balance, Good manager, 29–30
Limit setting:
with Bully manager, 13–14
with Parent manager, 176–177
Listening:
by Scientist manager, 111–112
by Seventh Leader, 201
to Star manager, 86
Litmus test (*See* Identification
questions)
Little Tyrant manager, 189–190
Logic (*See* Analytical and logical)
Loyalty:
to organization, 110–111
to Scientist manager, 102–103, 110–111
to Star manager, 88–89

M

Manager archetypes:
Bully, 1–25
Con Artist, 183–187
Geek, 177–180
Good, 27–49
Kaleidoscope, 51–72
Laisser-Aller, 171–174
Little Tyrant, 189–190
Navel, 119–140
Number 2, 180–183
Parent, 174–177
Perfectionist, 188–189
Scientist, 97–118
Star manager, 73–95
Managing your manager:
benefits of, xxvii–xxix
challenges of, xxv–xxvii
identifying type, 187–190
need for understanding, xv–xvi,
xxv–xxvii
questions to know manager, xxvi–
xxvii
(*See also* Secret strategies to manage
your manager; *specific topics*)
Manipulative and calculating behavior:
by Bully manager, 6

by Kaleidoscope manager, 51–72
of Navel manager, 131–132
Matrix management structure, 17, 103,
166
Micromanagement:
by Bully manager, 4
by Parent manager, 175–176
Mistakes:
by Navel manager, 122–123
and Scientist manager, 102
Moderation, Good manager, 34
Multiple managers, challenge of
knowing, xxv–xxvi

N

Navel manager, 119–140
actions and behaviors, 121–123
asking for promotion, 159–160
becoming the Seventh Leader,
213–214
biggest challenge for, 213–214
crisis situation, 148–149
the Don'ts, 133–136
feedback process, 201
identification questions, 124–127
interpersonal tactics, 127–130
positive achievement, 153–154
potential to become Seventh Leader,
213–214
professional tactics, 130–133
risky-but-needed decisions, 164–165
secret strategy, 139–140
telling traits, 124–127
tolerance assessment, 136–138
Naysayer, and the Star manager, 89–90
Networking, for Good manager, 38–39
Number 1 manager, learning details
about, 182
Number 2 manager, 180–183
Number 3, avoiding becoming,
182–183

P

Pandering, with Good manager,
44
Parent manager, 174–177

Gonzague Dufour is a human resources executive who has held senior executive positions with top companies such as Bacardi, Phillip Morris, Kraft, Jacobs Suchard, and consulting firms. During this time, he has worked in Eastern Europe, the Middle East, Africa, Latin America, Canada, France, and the United States in various executive HR capacities. Besides HR, he has worked in the area of mergers, acquisitions, leadership, and change management. He joined Bacardi in 2009 and currently resides in Larchmont, New York.